ENDORSEMENTS

We all need wisdom on how to lead in a more healthy and productive way. This book, written by Mark Ramsey along with one of his key leaders, Karolina Gunsser, breaks down practically all that is needed to create a culture of health and strength within the people we lead. The leadership culture that Mark and Leigh Ramsey have built at Citipointe Church is like few in the world today. The health, individuality, creativity and broad generational expression they have achieved are the result of their tried and true leadership practices. Congratulations, Mark, Leigh and Karolina! I am excited for a broader audience to be able to learn the principles and secrets that have enabled Citipointe to produce such a healthy and strong leadership culture.

Leanne Matthesius
Senior Pastor
Awaken Church Americas

I have known Mark for many years and can attest to his unwavering pursuit to love God and love people. He champions the Church of Jesus Christ, is a builder of people and a faithful friend. I believe his leadership teaching and wisdom will release potential and purpose within every reader and will inspire you to become the leader God has called you to be.

Brian Houston
Global Senior Pastor
Hillsong Church

Pastor Mark Ramsey has been a friend of ours for many years. He is a man with passion and humility who lives out servant-hearted leadership. I believe this book is both timely and necessary.

Lisa Bevere
New York Times bestselling author of
Without Rival and *Girls with Swords*

Leading is not easy. Leading at multiple levels is harder. Most leaders who are not at the top of their organisations give up or don't even try. My friends Pastors Mark Ramsey and Karolina Gunsser have written a book that debunks the one-way paradigm and encourages healthy leadership at all levels and directions. *Expanded Leadership* needs to be a must-read for leaders in every Christian organisation at every level.

Sam Chand
Leadership Consultant and author of
New Thinking, New Future

EXPANDED
LEADERSHIP

Growing beyond one-dimensional leadership

Mark Ramsey and Karolina Gunsser

Unless otherwise noted, all Scripture quotations are from the New King James Version®. Copyright © 1982 by Thomas Nelson. Used by permission. All rights reserved.

Scripture quotations marked (NLT) are taken from the Holy Bible, New Living Translation. Copyright ©1996, 2004, 2015 by Tyndale House Foundation. Used by permission of Tyndale House Publishers, Carol Stream, Illinois 60188. All rights reserved.

Scripture quotations marked ESV are taken from The ESV® Bible (The Holy Bible, English Standard Version®). Copyright © 2001 by Crossway, a publishing ministry of Good News Publishers. Used by permission. All rights reserved.

Scripture quotations marked MSG are taken from *The Message*. Copyright © 1993, 2002, 2018 by Eugene H. Peterson. Used by permission of NavPress. All rights reserved. Represented by Tyndale House Publishers, a Division of Tyndale House Ministries.

Scripture quotations marked TPT are from The Passion Translation®. Copyright © 2017, 2018 by Passion & Fire Ministries, Inc. Used by permission. All rights reserved. ThePassionTranslation.com.

Typesetting by Midland Typesetters, Australia
Art direction and design by Jess Steer, Citipointe Church
Edited by Rachael Tan

Printed in Australia by McPherson's Printing Group

ISBN 978–0–6451276–0–7

DEDICATION

Expanded Leadership is dedicated to the congregation, volunteers and staff of Citipointe Church, in appreciation and gratitude for growing with us for more than two decades now.

Let's together press in all the more and see more of Heaven come to earth so that more of earth can go to Heaven.

CONTENTS

PROLOGUE

KAROLINA GUNSSER

I was eighteen years old when I walked into Citipointe Church for the first time. It was a big place, and I wanted to remain another face in the crowd. I was a broken, up-side-down girl searching for meaning.

Pastor Mark Ramsey preached that night. I came back the following week and the week after that, and every week since then.

I found healing quietly, hidden among the crowd. Eventually, I signed up to the choir and joined a small group where I would meet my husband, Sam.

At the age of nineteen, I was surprised to hear from Pastor Mark's assistant. I was invited to give the offering message in the Sunday services. Apparently, word had reached him that I had done a good job speaking in the Youth Ministry where Sam and I were serving, and he put my name on the preaching roster for Sunday.

Since that time, Pastor Mark has drawn potential out of me. He has identified gifting in me that I did not know was there. He has defended me, opened doors for me, invited my input and celebrated me beyond any expectation I could have held for myself. He has been the greatest of leaders.

It has been twenty years since that first night at Citipointe Church. Sam and I now lead one of the locations in our multi-site Church. Sam and I are raising four children, have trained and released countless leaders and pastors, have thrived and seen others thrive and have been encouraged and released time and time again to step into the calling of God on our lives.

There is a synergy that happens when the generations under-stand the dynamic nature of interconnectedness. We see it all the way through Scripture. Ruth and Naomi were mutually (and exceedingly) blessed through their commitment and loyalty to one another's success. As were Paul and Timothy, Moses and Joshua and many others.

The principle is this: a spiritual, generational transference takes place when fathers and sons, mothers and daughters, fight for each other. The Kingdom of Heaven is a generational one. It requires a resolve to loyalty, and it is a pathway to blessing.

I once heard a statement that has held me in true stead:

> **"THERE IS SOMETHING WRONG WITH YOUR CHARACTER IF OPPORTUNITY CONTROLS YOUR LOYALTY."**[1]

Never in a million years did I expect to be co-authoring this book with the man I heard preach all those years ago. I often say that God was kind when He led me into the auditorium that night.

I do not take lightly the care Pastors Mark and Leigh Ramsey have given me and my family, the room they have made and the pride they have shown in Sam and me. I am keenly aware of the trust and faith they have sown into the soil of my life—the risk they took on this girl. They created a space for me.

Sitting in their shade allowed me to heal and hope again, or maybe for the first time—I am not sure. Over time, I gained the courage to speak, and they allowed me to weigh in, surprised to be called out of the shadows and given a voice. Standing by their side allowed me to dare to dream again. They allowed me to learn at my own pace, and they trusted that process.

As I stepped into greater measures of the potential being drawn out of me, I found a deeper call to lead.

This book is all about this gracious expression of leadership according to God's plan. When Heaven's sons and daughters, fathers and mothers, understand the interconnection they have to each other through the Spirit, they walk in a realm of grace and blessing that is unrivalled.

Whoever you are, wherever you are in the process, you are called to influence. Your influence spans far wider than you imagine, and its effects can be felt in the generations on either side of you. My prayer for you as you read this book is that you find your grounding, that you hear the Spirit's whispers over your potential and that you take up the challenge to become an expanded leader. It's the best ride!

This is our offering to you—enjoy!

Karolina Gunsser

CHAPTER 1:

DISPELLING THE MYTH

MARK RAMSEY AND KAROLINA GUNSSER

One of the young men in our Church enlisted in the army a few years ago and was accepted. Being quite a cheeky, sarcastic sort of guy, we were hoping they would train it out of him. But they didn't. Being back with us now, he is still a loveable larrikin. Sharing his experience, he assures us that so much of what people see in the movies is actually true. They give the new recruits an extremely hard time. These men and women literally sleep with one eye open. They awake in the morning to a Corporal yelling, "HALLWAY!" followed by their platoon number. The recruits respond by echoing the shout and running to the hallway to stand at attention while being yelled and sworn at. They are told to tuck their bed sheets in properly at the corners, or the sheets get ripped off, and they have to start again. They keep the new recruits on their toes every second of every day for no reason except to break them down so they can build them up again according to the code of the army. Strip them down to bare basics and remould them into whatever it is the army believes they need to be.

Before going into the mess hall where they eat their meals, the new recruits were ordered not to eat dessert to assure they would pass their upcoming Physical Fitness Assessment (PFA). Each night, dessert was put in front of them, but they were not allowed to eat it. The other soldiers who passed their PFA enjoyed dessert, but the new recruits were not allowed to touch it.

During the day, they went through intensive classes. One of these classes was on the Military Law system and how it works. The new recruit realised that it was unlawful to be told that he wasn't allowed to have something for which he had already paid. Well, this friend of ours, who is not the kind of person to tolerate that sort of thing for very long, started eating his dessert after the class. A Corporal officer patrolling the mess hall confronted him and ordered him to report to his Platoon's admin line for a verbal dressing down after dessert.

Once he had happily finished his dessert, our friend arrived at the Platoon's admin line, and the Corporal began the dressing down, "What do you think you're doing? You have been ordered not to eat the dessert!"

This young friend of ours began explaining, "We have been taught Military Law, and your order was unlawful." He continued, "I pay $150 a week for food, so I'm going to eat my dessert." The Corporal continued the barrage, causing the recruit to start laughing, which only infuriated the Corporal further.

What was interesting is that the Platoon Lieutenant overheard what was happening from his office and came out laughing to himself. He told the young private that while he was correct, he could have shown more respect for the chain of command. Needless to say, the Platoon Lieutenant allowed all the young privates to eat dessert from that point.

The young private told more stories from his experience, but one story stands out from the rest. One of the intensive classes was an afternoon leadership session.

The Platoon Lieutenant posed a question to the group, "What is leadership?"

As the question went around the room, each young private answered the question the best way they could, with mostly textbook answers.

"Leadership is influence." "Leadership is delegation." "Leadership is authority." "Leadership is power."

When it came to our friend, he began to explain the four types of leadership. "There are those you are *responsible over*," which was the only type of leadership that all the other young recruits were describing. "You are also *responsible with* your peers. You are *responsible to* your bosses and superiors. And you are *responsible for* yourself, which is the most important form of leadership," he said.

At that point, the Platoon Lieutenant stopped the conversation and dismissed the privates. "We are done here for today," he said. "You can all go."

But he detained our friend for further discussion. "Where did you learn that?" the Platoon Lieutenant insisted.

"I learnt it in Church," he replied. "It's how we talk about leadership. That's what we believe as Christians."

At that moment, he was granted an opportunity to talk about Kingdom culture in a worldly code and a worldly system. His Platoon Lieutenant had never in his whole career met a young man coming into the army who understood what this young private could articulate about leadership.

As evidenced by this young man's experience among his peers, there is a limited understanding among many that suggest leading is one-dimensional. To break this myth and open our minds to an expanded form of leadership is to counter the trend of common thinking.

In an effort to expand our perspective of what it looks like to lead effectively, we will come to understand four different dimensions of leadership and discover the necessity of becoming an expanded leader in each of these four dimensions.

It does not matter what position or role you have; there is always an element of leadership involved. In fact, as a baseline, it is significant to recognise that if you are a follower of Jesus, you are immediately called to influence. You cannot be a believer without some degree of leadership that emanates from your life. We are called to be cities on hills and light in dark places.[1] We are called to impact our culture and generation in positive ways.

As soon as you become a believer, there will be a leadership aspect to your life. From the everyday Jesus follower, the trades-person, the homemaker, the corporate professional, to the CEO and politician, every one of us has an influence on the world around us.

Unfortunately, we all have blind spots. The problem with blind spots is that we do not know what they are. That is why we call them blind spots. Identifying them could be the difference between greater capacity, breaking barriers, reaching goals or falling short of fulfilling your vision and mission. Deep within us lies the full ingredient list for effective leadership. Sadly, many fall short because they are unaware of their own blind spots. The failure to understand that there are more than one or two dimensions to leadership affects countless leaders.

Jesus, in Matthew 10, reveals an often-overlooked understanding of influence that we each can have and ascribes an eternal weight to each one.

> "He who receives a prophet in the name of a ***prophet*** shall receive a prophet's reward. And he who receives a ***righteous man*** in the name of a righteous man shall receive a righteous man's reward. And whoever gives

one of these **little ones** only a cup of cold water in the name of a disciple, assuredly, I say to you, he shall by no means lose his reward."

(Matthew 10:41–42, emphasis added)

Through Jesus, we learn there are interactions in various spheres of our human experience, which impact the heart of God according to our responses.

Below is a graphic and brief summary of this expanded view of leadership.

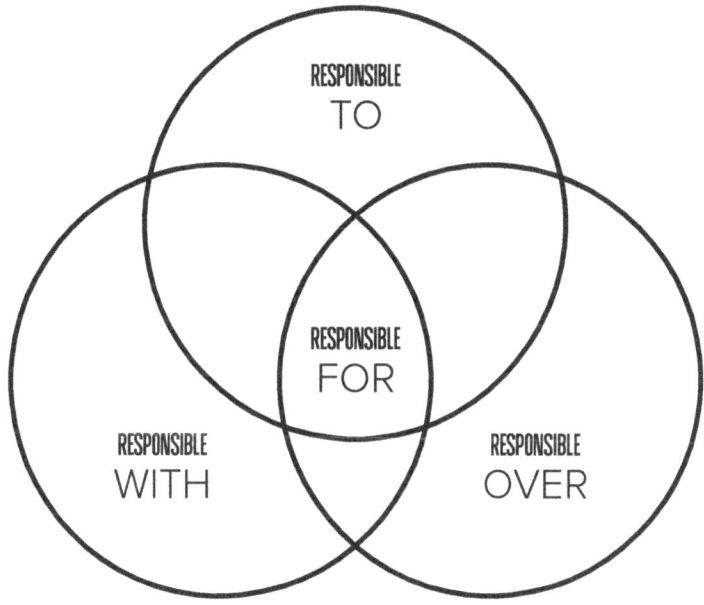

Here, the three spheres of influence are clearly seen; the fourth is perhaps less obvious while underscoring them all.

We are *responsible over* the teams we lead and those entrusted to our care. In the context of Jesus' description in Matthew 10, these are the "little ones"—those in our care, under our authority.

As well as being a great leader of your own teams, can you effectively lead your peers? In Jesus' reference, our peers are the "righteous" ones on either side of us. These are the people we are *responsible with*.

Do you have the ear of your superiors because you are dynamic in your understanding of the influence you carry on those you are *responsible to*? Jesus called these ones "prophets"—those who carry authority over us and who we are led by and answerable to.

In the centre of this diagram, you notice the most important leadership call: the ability to lead one's self. The only person we are ever *responsible for* is ourselves. God's main concern for us relates to the condition of our hearts. Is your current success as a leader sustainable, and is your future development ensured through a commitment and ability to lead yourself?

There is no shortage of literature and teaching resources on leadership. Most often, the focus of these teachings is "down-ward leadership" to those we are responsible over. The truth is, however, that there is more than one dimension of leadership.

The ability to be *responsible over* teams has propelled many into the leadership stratosphere; it has unearthed countless promising leaders, and it has seen the realisation of goals and team missions right throughout history. However, this form of leadership alone has a limited reach. It is just one of four dimensions of leadership. The first three dimensions are cited in the passage above; the fourth undergirds them all and is of primary concern to God.

In his book, *The 360 Degree Leader*, John Maxwell extensively defines the first three dimensions of leadership. Maxwell aptly describes these leadership influences as Leading Down, Leading Across and Leading Up.[2]

Expanded Leadership will show how leaders must exercise a commitment to these three distinct and unique groups of people, then also recognise the importance of leading one's self as the precursor and foundation of all leadership. A leader who will continue to grow and reach new heights must harness expanded leadership ability. Failure to do so will restrict the reach of that leader, bringing them to a plateau, or worse, an eventual decline in their effectiveness and ability to lead.

If you want to reach great heights as a leader, you need to expand your reach to become a multi-dimensional leader. This means your growth and sustained impact will depend on your ability to lead a broad array of audiences.

Through close observation, we can quickly recognise that truly dynamic and long-term leaders have harnessed their abilities in each of these four dimensions. Each of these functions is interwoven through the fabric of a strong leader; their successful practice and deployment determine how far that leader will extend.

There are many leaders cited in the pages of the Bible who flourished in these four dimensions, and there are many who didn't; we will explore their examples. We will also reflect on personal and anecdotal experiences from the leadership experiences we have gained in the last twenty years of Citipointe Church.

IF YOU WANT TO REACH GREAT HEIGHTS AS A LEADER, YOU NEED TO EXPAND YOUR REACH TO BECOME A MULTI-DIMENSIONAL LEADER.

Our hope is that this book will help you identify the following:

- » How to strengthen the four dimensions of leadership.
- » Which of the four dimensions you may not be utilising effectively yet.
- » The tools you need to grow in each of the four dimensions of leadership.

Contained in these pages are bite-sized concepts that you can take and readily apply to your leadership practice or work through with teams of volunteers and employees.

Perhaps this book will help answer some real questions you or your team have held about how to grow as leaders. That is our goal: to see you expand and reach your full potential and to equip you to lead effectively in every setting.

Before we delve into the four dimensions of leadership, let us first consider a few basic truths that should be applied across each of the four settings. A great leader will remember the following fundamental attitudes in their environments and encounters with all types of people. They are, in essence, the leader's "Rules of Engagement."

CHAPTER 2:

RULES OF ENGAGEMENT

MARK RAMSEY

Integrity. You may have heard it said that integrity is the ability to live with nothing to prove and nothing to hide. It means that we are the same person in office corridors as we are in the spotlight. On the platform and off the platform, we are true and consistent. We do not change depending on the situation or the company.

While this book will deal with different settings and the four receptive audiences within our leadership reach, first and fore-most, we must commit to being consistent in whichever encounter we find ourselves. Without a commitment to integrity, you may fool others for a while, but when your true colours begin to show, and inevitably they will, your leadership credibility will be proportionately affected.

Whether you are relating to your boss, your peers or a member of the team you lead, consider and adopt the following "Rules of Engagement" as a set of functional attitudes that will serve as your compass for interactions. A great leader will remember the following six fundamental attitudes in their environments and encounters with all types of people.

FOCUSED BUT KIND

There is no room for rudeness in the Kingdom of God and, therefore, no room for rudeness in the demeanour of a leader who is a follower of Jesus.

Will people upset you? Absolutely.
Will they let you down? Yes.
At times will they deserve your disapproval? More than likely.

But playing the role of judge and jury is not the job of a Christian leader.[1] We are called to maintain our focus without being rude, even in the face of pressure and disappointment.

There is no doubt we need to get the job done. We are on a mission from God. People's lives and eternities are counting on us. Yet, even a laser focus on the task at hand should never negate the necessity to soften our voices and pad out our sentences. In our fast-paced world of emails and text messages, a great deal of kindness and good intent is lost in translation. Remember to slow down enough so you can maintain a gentle etiquette. It can be as simple as opening with a greeting and closing with thanks. Extra effort and a smiley emoticon can go a long way to preserving morale and high spirits among team members.

In God's Kingdom, we are not rude people. We want to make sure that people feel inspired, welcomed and a part of the plan when they interact with us, whether it is through a text, email, phone call or in person.

Unfortunately, some people mistake rudeness for strength. Rudeness is not strength. Rudeness is just rudeness. On the flip side, some people mistake kindness for weakness. Not so.

Kindness is not being weak; kindness is godly and one of the fruits of the Spirit.

Jesus Himself taught us that the meek are blessed and can expect a great inheritance. Meekness, humility and kindness are signs of maturity and strength.

> "Blessed are the meek,
>
> For they shall inherit the earth."

(Matthew 5:5)

Kindness moves us forward politely. Kindness makes tough decisions respectfully. We should not avoid making tough decisions; we should just make them with humility and in the best way possible.

BOLD BUT INCLUSIVE

Our boldness in making tough decisions should use sensitivity to remain open to the input of others.

NOWHERE IN THE BIBLE DOES IT SAY THAT WE ARE TO LIVE BY SECURITY.

Bold people win the day. You have to take risks and take them boldly. Faith is essential to fulfil God's plan. Nowhere in the Bible does it say that we are to live by security. Quite the opposite—we are called to live by faith. According to the writers of Romans, Galatians and Hebrews, living by faith is the signature of righteous living.

> "The righteous shall live by faith."

(Romans 1:17, Galatians 3:11 ESV)

> "My righteous one shall live by faith."

(Hebrews 10:38 ESV)

You do not have to lead for very long to realise that faith is spelled R-I-S-K. Faith requires risk and trust in God. It also requires boldness.

If you exercise a leadership function within a Church context, pause for a moment and consider the job that you do. You sell a "product" that cannot be seen by enlisting help from people you do not pay. What an impossible task you have decided to undertake! Kingdom leadership takes faith; it takes boldness.

In our boldness, we should never be so far ahead of our team that they can no longer see us. We must remain together. When you sound the charge, be sure that you do not run so far ahead of the rest that they pull back and relax while you get the job done alone. Do not be so in charge, so in control, so overbearing that your team leaves the work to you or, worse still, become afraid of taking their own initiative.

Great leaders know how to stand at the front while still making others feel valued and respected as co-labourers. As a leader, you have envisaged, meditated, strategised and then communicated your vision with the team. People take time to catch up, so give them the space to do so. Make sure you are an inclusive leader.

An additional strength of any great leader is their ability to create a world so large that it has the capacity to include big-thinking, high-achieving people within it—people with big opinions and big ideas. They need to be sought out, welcomed and encouraged on the team. The thing that keeps most churches and organisations small is a leader who is intimidated by big people. Unintentionally, they force big people away. They do not mean to, but they create a small world where there is no room for ideas,

GREAT LEADERS KNOW HOW TO STAND AT THE FRONT WHILE STILL MAKING OTHERS FEEL VALUED AND RESPECTED AS CO-LABOURERS.

initiative or creativity other than their own. This does not mean that ideas and opinions that are contrary to God's Word need to be embraced, but a wise leader can speak and lead in such situations without making others feel small or belittled.

Build your team. Listen. Welcome opinions. Earn respect. Utilise gifts and talents. Then, you will become a leader who is bold and achieves the tasks while including great people along the way.

HUMBLE NOT TIMID

You cannot achieve significant goals if you are timid. You have got to step out of the proverbial boat from time to time. In fact, most of the miracles that will happen in your life will take place after you have stepped out of your boat of fear, mediocrity, intimidation, preference, complacency or whatever else it may be.

When Jesus' disciples saw Him walking on water towards them that fateful night, they were all faced with the same opportunity. Yet, only one of the twelve overcame his fear and stepped out of the boat in response to Jesus' beckoning. Peter is famous for walking on water while the other eleven remained in the security and familiarity of the boat.[2]

Miracles happen outside our comfort zones. You cannot be timid. Dynamic leadership demands that you step up and step out. The Apostle Paul urges us to remember that fear is not our portion in God. In fact, we have a spirit opposite to fear.

MIRACLES HAPPEN OUTSIDE OUR COMFORT ZONES.

> For God has not given us a spirit of fear, but of power and of love and of a sound mind.

(2 Timothy 1:7)

Some translations interchange the term "sound mind" with "self-discipline." Sometimes you have to tell your mind what to think and discipline it into following with necessary action.

We are called to avoid fear, double-mindedness and poor commitment at all costs.[3] We need faith. We need courage. We need confidence.

Not all leaders are naturally self-confident people. But we can all possess a keen sense of "God-confidence." This means we can be confident and stand strong in the midst of challenges, not because of what we believe about ourselves but because of *who* we believe. Our confidence does not come from the past or the picture we have of the future but from God, who is present through it all and calling us towards the goal. It is a humble confidence.

It is important for us to cultivate a belief system that understands humility is not the same as timidity. Often, we use the word *humble* interchangeably with the word *timid*, which is an entirely wrong concept. While timid people rarely step out of their boats, humble people lean on a strength greater than themselves and obey the call.

A humble person knows they do not need to prove themselves.

A HUMBLE PERSON KNOWS THEY DO NOT NEED TO PROVE THEMSELVES.

Your greatest season of growth in leadership comes when you get past the point of thinking you have to prove yourself or that you somehow have to show the world who you are. As soon as you pass that mindset, you can step easily into the strength of humility.

Humility declares, "I do not need to prove myself. I am willing to do whatever it takes. I am willing to change." Humility is being secure in who we are and in God who calls us.

If we look a little closer, we will admit that the antithesis of humility is pride. However, we should not be fooled; pride is not always as obnoxious as we may think. It can be much more subtle than outward gloating about status or possessions. Pride is often an inability or resistance to change.

We are made aware in Scripture that God willingly and joyfully gives grace to the humble; He also resists the proud.[4] We would all agree that the one person we do not wish to resist us would be God.

Who is a proud person? God is not necessarily talking about the boisterous show-offs. Pride is more often evident in a person who is not prepared to go through the often-uncomfortable growth processes required for change. It is the reason a whole generation perished in the wilderness, never seeing the Promised Land.

It is also the reason that many leaders today fall short of their ordained potential.

Humility is not a weakness, and it is not timidity. Humility shows itself in a person who knows who they are and who they are not. Humility knows who is in charge because it knows who God is in the equation. Humility ascribes appropriate authority and power to God. Humility submits to His beckoning and believes that through every challenge, He is the Source, the Author and the Finisher. Humility does not seek validation and is open to correction for growth and effectiveness.

Do not be timid—be brave! Be humble, teachable, pliable and willing to change through growth. Adopt a mindset that knows there is always something new to learn.

EXCELLENCE NOT ARROGANCE

Be the best you can be. Do not be scared of being rich, famous and brilliant. People wrongly avoid these blessings when God actually wants you to carry influence and be the best you can be. He is not intimidated by your success; He is glorified. You are blessed to be a blessing.

Your success is no threat to God. He is not intimidated by your brilliance or your stellar performance. In fact, you can be certain that nothing would bring Him more joy than to see you reach the heights of your calling, employing and deploying each of the talents and personality traits He intentionally placed within you.

Your success is not the issue, but developing arrogance is. The challenge to being successful is staying free of arrogance. The world does not model this well for us. Even the heroes of the Bible wrestled between humanity and arrogance. A brief character study of King Saul in the Old Testament cites perfectly for us that fame and influence can turn even the most timid of people into crazed, narcissistic power mongers. It is also important to note that influence is inevitably stripped from those who fall into this unhealthy pattern of leadership.

A Kingdom-oriented leader seeks to be the best they can be and carry presence and influence in their spheres without bragging or being self-promoting. Scripture prompts us to leave the conferral of praise to others while we focus on leading and influencing.

> Let another man praise you, and not your own mouth;
> A stranger, and not your own lips.

(Proverbs 27:2)

Influence should never come from position or title alone. You know when leaders are in trouble because they are the ones who find it necessary to remind everyone that they are in charge. "I'm the leader." "I'm the pastor." "I'm the boss." This is dangerous ground. As soon as you have resorted to those statements, you have fallen to the lowest form of leadership; you have lost credibility. You are now leading out of position rather than authority, trust and respect. Leading out of position is the lowest form of leadership.

> "BEING POWERFUL IS LIKE BEING A LADY.
> IF YOU HAVE TO TELL PEOPLE YOU ARE,
> YOU PROBABLY AREN'T."
>
> (MARGARET THATCHER)

Arrogance is the ugly offspring of the attitude that says, "Don't you know who I am?" It demands that people pay homage to a position. It may not be said out loud, but it is a common attitude that can fester within leaders who have lost sight of the main thing.

Arrogance carries with it a sense of entitlement. There is nothing wrong with privilege, but you should never expect it.

> Do not exalt yourself in the presence of the king,
> And do not stand in the place of the great;
> For it is better that he say to you,
> "Come up here,"
> Than that you should be put lower in the presence
> of the prince,
> Whom your eyes have seen.

(Proverbs 25:6–7)

When Citipointe Worship travels around the world, we receive encouraging reports from churches and events where they minister. Some of the churches they visit are ministries that we have had long-term friendships with that we cherish and hold dear. One common report that comes back to us is that the most enjoyable factor they experience is Citipointe Worship's heart to serve. There are no prima donnas. There are no attitudes of, "you can find me in my trailer." They are willing to serve, stay back, connect and add value wherever they go. That is what success without arrogance looks like.

We want to make sure we keep that attitude at all costs. Allow your success to speak for you, but always find your identity in Jesus, not position or accolades.

Titles are given, but respect is earned. A title offers you prominence, while respect paves the way for significance, and there is a world of difference between the two. Significance always carries longer-lasting influence than prominence.

SIGNIFICANCE ALWAYS CARRIES LONGER-LASTING INFLUENCE THAN PROMINENCE.

The desire for significance will push you towards success. The desire for prominence will push you towards arrogance. Arrogance will push you into selfishness and ultimately rob you of the call God has for your life. Again, King Saul sets a clear precedent for what happens when a leader's sense of influence becomes entitlement rather than privilege. The pathway of the arrogant diminishes swiftly. Authority is removed from the leader who has allowed God's intention and Kingdom influence to take a back seat to self.

You can be arrogant in the world and get away with it, but not in the Kingdom of God. It does not work well in God's economy, on His watch and in His purposes. God wants you to be successful, but He will resist you if you become arrogant.

HUMOUROUS AND WISE

A sense of humour is a great tool in leadership. It puts people at ease. Some of the biggest decisions we have navigated with our executive team have been approached with a sense of humour. When the leader can smile at adversity, the team is at ease and can be confident for the future. When the leader can laugh, the rest of the team feels that it is going to be all right.

Humour makes difficult concepts more easily palatable. It lends itself well in the art of communication. It makes messages easier to remember. It helps build bridges between people.

When you are speaking in front of new crowds, where the audience does not already know you, you only have a few minutes to build a relationship so that they are willing to listen to what you have to say. A great tactic is to use humour.

If I were a song leader, I would just sing to build rapport with people. But in my present reality, that would not help me build relationships. In fact, it would work in the opposite way. It would be funny, but it would err on the edge of foolishness, not humour.

There was a time many years ago when Leigh and I were pastoring our first Church in Noosa, Australia, and I left my microphone switched on while worshipping in the Spirit. The recording was duplicated on cassette tape back then and became my largest selling cassette of the year.

Humour lightens dark moments. Going through my cancer treatment in 2011, I certainly turned to humour to lighten many moments in that season. Even now, when I speak about that time in my life, or when I spend time with people on that journey themselves, I like to bring a sense of light through humour to that narrative. When they see me laugh, they can see the darkness through my lighter perspective, and it gives them hope that they too are going to be okay.

You cannot let the enemy steal your joy, no matter what you are going through. "The joy of the Lord is your strength"

(Nehemiah 8:10). Of all the things you cannot afford to lose as a believer, your spiritual strength is extremely important. Joy is the source of that strength. So, humour becomes an effective tool in leadership at many levels.

However, if you cross a line, humour quickly ceases to be helpful and can become a hindrance.[5] When you go from funny to foolish, you lose credibility as a leader. If you do not want to be the leader, rest assured that there would always be a position for you as the class clown. People may laugh at you, but they will not follow you. Being funny, not foolish, is an important tension to manage as a leader.

OPTIMISTIC BUT GROUNDED

One of the greatest challenges in leadership is to remain true to the vision. A skill that very few people manage well is being able to see where they want to be and where they want to go while still living faithfully in their current reality. The gap between current reality and future goals can be discouraging at times. The difference between what you want and what you have, between what God has called you to do and where you are now, is the ground that leaders wrestle with on a daily basis.

You must be an optimist in the sense that although you are not "there" yet, you know that with God, you can and will someday be "there." While some believe it will all work out "no matter what," this mindset is neither strategic nor effective.

Words and confessions certainly carry power, but words only carry power if you believe them, not just because you confess them. If success were all about correct confessions, then parrots would rule the world. When we say, "confess the Word of God," the power is not in the word itself but rather the faith behind the words and the revelation that has brought renewed mindsets and behaviours.[6]

Many think that just by saying the right things, good things will work out. History is dotted with many pastors who have declared that they would "take their city for Jesus" but never planned or executed a strategy to bring their hopes to pass.

WE HAVE TO BE OPTIMISTS WITHOUT AVOIDING REALITY.

We do not need leaders who are blind optimists. Faith is not stupid or void. Faith is a risk, not a gamble. We have to be optimists without avoiding reality.

Others are so overcome by their reality that all they ever see are problems and lack, which cripples them to such an extent that they do not even bother trying. Skilful leadership is not avoiding problems or pretending they do not exist, or giving up before you start. Skilful leadership understands that with God, all things are possible and that we have to work the strategic plan.

Faith is not lazy, but it is at rest.[7] Faith does not take the work out of life; it takes the worry out of life.

We must remain optimistic and believe all God's promises to us while still accepting the necessary responses and actions to take us into those promises. No one promised us a leadership journey free from challenges, but God did promise that in the midst of those challenges, He would bring us forward.

WE CAN REMAIN OPTIMISTIC WHEN WE BELIEVE THAT DEEP WITHIN EVERY PROBLEM LIES ITS POTENTIAL SOLUTION.

We can remain optimistic when we believe that deep within every problem lies its potential solution. We are promised in Scripture that we have already been given all the things we need in this life to live the call we have been given. Therefore, we can confidently approach our challenges with a sense of expectation that with God on our side, we will find the strategy and operate from a position of victory.

> Grace and peace be multiplied to you in the knowledge of God and of Jesus our Lord, as His divine power has given to us all things that pertain to life and godliness, through the knowledge of Him who called us by glory and virtue...
>
> (2 Peter 1:2–3)

We need not become blind optimists nor suffer from analysis paralysis. Neither end of the spectrum is effective. Neither one is consistent with Heaven's perspective. What we need to become are leaders who move forward in faith, with a hope that points us in the right direction.

We should not spend more time setting up for survival in the desert than we do strategising our way out. Too many people are working out how to exist in their dysfunction rather than spending their energy exercising obedient faith to make a way out of it.

Optimism is a combination of faith and strategy. We confidently navigate our way to victory, not by avoiding problems but by rearranging and reimagining them through the wisdom and insight of the Holy Spirit.

Skilfully hone what God has given you as a leader, so you and those with you can be expanded and go to new levels.

OPTIMISM IS A COMBINATION OF FAITH AND STRATEGY.

Perhaps you have noticed already how subtle the attitude adjustments can be and just how vigilant we must all remain in keeping our hearts healthy as leaders. We can take a regular stocktake of our internal condition using checks like this. Playing by these rules will help you and your team enjoy the journey you are all on together.

Now that we have set some ground rules, we can delve into the subject matter at hand—how to expand our leadership reach to become multi-dimensional leaders.

PERSONAL REFLECTION:

Where have I taken myself too seriously?

Which one of these rules of engagement
have I most struggled with?

How can I address this particular area of my leadership?

What is my biggest fear in leading people?

PART ONE:

LEADING THOSE I AM
RESPONSIBLE OVER

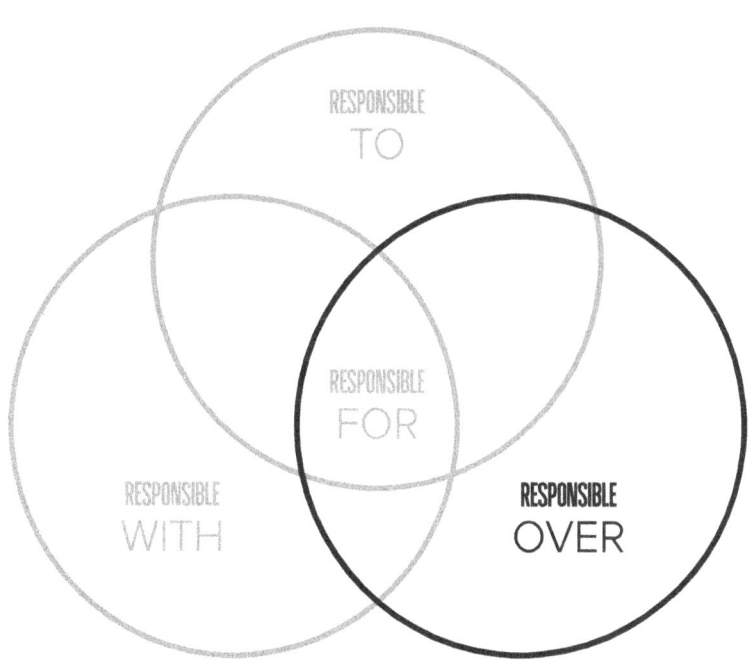

(1 PETER 5:2−4 ^{NLT})

Care for the flock that God has entrusted to you. Watch over it willingly, not grudgingly—not for what you will get out of it, but because you are eager to serve God. Don't lord it over the people assigned to your care, but lead them by your own good example. And when the Great Shepherd appears, you will receive a crown of never-ending glory and honour.

"You will get all you want in life,
if you help enough other people
get what they want."

— ZIG ZIGLAR

CHAPTER 3:

RESPONSIBLE OVER

MARK RAMSEY

Leadership is about getting things done and being *responsible over* people. These are the people who fill the teams we lead; they are our subordinates and assistants. This is a significant aspect of leadership. It is through this dimension that we achieve our organisational goals most commonly due to a team effort. Leaders coordinate, enthuse and manage people. Good leaders know what has to be done, have a plan, and coordinate people and resources to accomplish the task.

An industrious team meets objectives according to directives. This is the most common form of leadership. The notion of leadership in this context is usually seen as someone standing out front leading a team towards an end goal. Yet, there is another side to this dimension of leadership that is significantly important.

To be a leader in the Kingdom of God, you must not only stand out the front and direct those you are *responsible over*, but you must also commit to serving the team you lead. In other words, a leadership position is not a title; it is a responsibility. It is not an elevated position within the hierarchy; it is simply a function within the overall team. Someone has to lead, and that someone holds the greatest responsibility on behalf of everyone else.

As the Global Senior Pastor of Citipointe Church, I do not see my role as more privileged than any other. I hold a place on the team just like everyone else. My position in our team is to help lead our Church into its future. Leading our team requires that I take on the role of a servant with those around me and that I foster a deep commitment to serving each of them.

When we run our individual races and stand before God to give an account, His welcome will hopefully sound something like, "Well done, good and faithful servant".[1] He will not say, "Well done, good and faithful preacher, worship leader or CEO." The highest calling we can hold is to serve. In fact, the pathway to greatness is through serving.

> "Yet it shall not be so among you; but whoever desires to become great among you, let him be your servant. And whoever desires to be first among you, let him be your slave."
>
> (Matthew 20:26–27)

Jesus was not saying that He wanted us to shrink back and avoid being great. The opposite is true. He was teaching us how to become great, and that is through serving. In other words, He was saying, become a servant—care about other people more than yourself—that is the pathway to greatness.

Each new cohort of Citipointe interns is ripe with enthusiasm and keen with anticipation for personal expansion. They commit for one year to be exclusively stretched, challenged and developed. Young and old alike, they are contagious with their excitement. Over twelve months, they facilitate entire Church portfolios—

developing and leading their teams to accomplish the portfolios' requirements. As soon as we can, we teach these new recruits that true leadership is about others.

We teach them that the essential requirement of shifting from self-focused leadership to Kingdom-focused leadership is a subtle but vital adjustment in a leader's perspective and attitude towards people. Leaders must become vigilant against using people for personal gain and committed instead to empowering them towards their individual callings in God.[2]

CHAPTER 4:

EMPOWER PEOPLE

MARK RAMSEY

It is important to understand that we have two options: we can either use people or we can empower people. To have an attitude that just commands and gives orders is not how the Kingdom of God works. This Kingdom of Heaven is not about a leader having a group of people running around after them and their wishes. The difference between using people and empowering them lies deep within our agendas and motivations for doing what we do.

WE CAN EITHER USE PEOPLE OR WE CAN EMPOWER PEOPLE.

You empower your team when you have an attitude that is committed to their potential. The good news is that other people benefit from being involved in the cause because it creates an avenue for them to deploy their gifts and abilities and reach their potential. While leaders need dedicated co-labourers to achieve the organisations' goals, each individual benefits greatly from the growth and exposure they experience within the team and the mission. It is a win-win scenario for both the leader and the follower.

You are saying to that person, "Even though we have a task to accomplish, we are working together, and I believe that you will be a better person at the end of it. You will learn skills, you will grow, you will be stronger, and you will go places. You will find a sense of value and personal betterment for being a part of this."

We want our team members to believe that they will find a sense of their own personal calling while connecting themselves to the cause we are leading. We desire them to stand up one day in the future and say, "Thank God I was involved in this mission and on this team."

We never want to be leaders who use people. The attitude behind using people says, "I need you to get what I want done. Once the task is accomplished and my need for you is satisfied, I will most likely no longer be interested in you." Although this is rarely explicitly communicated, we have all seen or experienced this and its effects by some leaders.

The result of this attitude is that team members are very visible and celebrated when they are needed, but otherwise, they are invisible when the leader no longer requires them. That, in essence, is exploitation. That should never happen in the Kingdom of God.

We want to be known as leaders who empower people and release them into their potential. People need to walk away from encounters with us feeling better about life. They need to be trained and equipped for every area to which they are called.

The skills that our volunteers learn through their involvement in Church are extraordinary and help develop them and set them up for life.

It is quite remarkable that one of the largest budget items in our Church every year is run by teenagers. Our annual youth camp is one of the largest ticket items on our calendar, and young people run it. Where else can a young person learn the types of skills to pull off an event of that scale, but in the House of God? The opportunities given to young volunteers every year in coordinating youth camp involve scheduling, budgeting, creative direction, networking, promotions, team building, recruiting, pastoral care, and the list goes on. They are volunteers and are investing generously of their time and personal efforts towards a corporate mission, but they are growing and learning skills along the way. Likewise, any other person who understands their position in the Church knows they are not just fulfilling a function but that they are contributing to an eternal cause, as well as learning to become a bigger person for their future.

A leader can be confident that approaching people with the prospect of becoming involved with Kingdom purposes is not a selfish motive. It is so much more than simply having an agenda met. We are part of the greatest cause on earth, and therefore, we can believe emphatically that when others are involved in Kingdom purposes, they will become bigger, better and stronger. We can come from a place of conviction that believes, "When I ask anybody to be involved, I know that they will be better off for accepting my invitation."

With this as a premise for Christian leadership, we resolutely believe that we do not use people in the Kingdom of God; we empower people. We are motivated by their potential and not simply furthering our own agenda. It becomes about the person, more than the task.

Part of empowering our team is genuinely caring about the people who are helping us carry out the call of God. Make sure that you know them, celebrate their personal milestones, encourage them and speak into their future. While we move forward getting things done, we need to empower people along the road to accomplishing the mission together. Serving the team in this way is a thrill and an honour. This is the mark of a great leader.

The person you are leading is more important than the task, and because you understand your call to empower people, not use them, this approach will have positive implications for team growth, morale and longevity.

As leaders of teams, we need to be cautious never to lead from a position or attitude that says, "Get this done because I said so, and I'm the boss." Instead, we understand that together is stronger. As mentioned in the Rules of Engagement, if you have to remind people of your position, you have actually lost credibility. The lowest form of leadership is to use the "boss card."

When you lead with an attitude of empowering people, your approach is totally different. You see them as significant and important, and as a result, their unique future is a priority to you.

EMPOWERING SOMEBODY REQUIRES AN UNDERSTANDING OR CONVICTION OF PARTNERSHIP.

In other words, empowering somebody requires an understanding or conviction of partnership. It is not only about "getting the boss's stuff done," but also about developing the members of the team along the way so that the seed of Heaven within them is activated to grow, and they meet their potential. Both win.

As leaders, we hold the power to control and command activity, but we also have the ability to connect individuals to the call of God on their lives. That is one of our God-given responsibilities. We are motivated and invigorated by helping others with their futures. A great leader understands that their true success depends on the success of the people they are leading.

Be assured, people who feel valued will always reach above and beyond the checklists and bare minimum of their jobs. People who get used will burn out, but people who are valued will go the extra mile.

The reality of the Church world is that many of us work with teams of volunteers. The Kingdom of God is significantly staffed by a workforce who do not receive financial compensation for their time and invest- ment. Our teams are made up of the heroic types that have received a revelation of discipleship that shifts their behaviour from consumers to con- tributors. They see the grand scheme of God's intentions in the earth and the eternal ramifications. They have

A GREAT LEADER UNDERSTANDS THAT THEIR TRUE SUCCESS DEPENDS ON THE SUCCESS OF THE PEOPLE THEY ARE LEADING.

understood, by the Holy Spirit's grace, that they can and should play a part in bringing Heaven to earth so that more of earth can go to Heaven.

They know that their reward is not only here in this life, in the faces of the lives that their efforts reach, but in a greater measure on the other side of eternity where our sight cannot yet clearly see.

When you empower somebody by asking them to be involved in what God has called you to accomplish, you know without hesitation that the best thing for their personal development is to be involved in the mission. The mission has gripped and grown you personally, and you are confident the same can be true for them. You know that if the person becomes involved, they will become a bigger, better and stronger person as a result.

Everybody wins in this scenario, and the Kingdom of Heaven extends. The leader accomplishes a goal, and the team member is developed and enlarged by being involved in the process of accomplishing the goal. Then, once the task is met, the leader does not isolate or discard them because they are understood to be a grand part of the Kingdom, and their place within it is valued. They are treasured as a child of God and celebrated as such. There has been a genuine bond formed between two mutual co-labourers on a worthy mission. This is a unifying bond that truly has no end date or project timeline.

Through this leadership role, we outwork our business model— the thing that God has called us to do. We have goals to achieve, budgets to work within, and we need to ensure that the mission is being accomplished. Good leadership is being clear on exactly what those goals are, what our targets are along the way and the strategies our team will employ to meet them. It requires a clear idea of where we are heading. In turn, it is important to understand that we need to involve other people and broader teams of people in order to arrive at the desired destination.

I often tell the story of going fishing off the coast of Queensland, Australia, at Fraser Island. A few years back, I was there with a group of friends, and we were out a fair way from the shore on a sandbank. Other than my brother Brad and a few others, there were quite a few guys I didn't know personally among the group we were with. We caught a lot of fish that day. When you catch Taylor—the type of fish we were bringing in—you cut their throats quickly, bleed them in the water and throw them into a sack on your back and cast out your line again and repeat. We did not notice the water rise as the tide was coming in. With the rising water, the dead fish hanging on our backs started to float in the water. There was so much blood in the water that we looked around and agreed that perhaps it was time to go back to shore. Just as we commenced to head back to the shore, we spotted an enormous fin in the water; all the blood in the water had attracted a big shark. The dilemma was that he could swim all the way around us as we stood on the sandbank and the water rose, so we were, in a way, cut off. Let me tell you, you have never seen a group of men get so close together. The reason being that everyone there knew that the inside position was the safest, and the shark was more likely to take the person positioned on the outside. Together, as one unit, we were able to shuffle back to the beach and back to safety.

I dread the thought of being out there that day by myself. Together is stronger.

ACT CONSISTENTLY

MARK RAMSEY

"BEING" IS THE SIGNATURE OF YOUR SOUL.

A leader has no greater power than their example. "Being" is the signature of your soul. Your example, your "being," is what you really believe on display. It is who you are, and consistency is the fuel that keeps that example lit. A leader's example empowers those following.

People follow those who act consistently. Great leaders lead by example; they embody the type of person they want others to be. For some of us, that might mean becoming what or who we wish someone had been for us. It always requires that we personally become the effectual change we want to see transpiring around us.

If we are different in the pulpit than we are in person, we lose credibility as leaders. Inconsistency diminishes the strength of our leadership, and the same goes for all of us. The moment people learn that a leader is not dependable or responsible is the moment they will no longer acknowledge that person's leadership.

Proverbs 20:6 tells us that many people will shout about their own greatness and that it is rare to find someone who is faithful and true to his word. Five chapters later, Proverbs 25:14 says, "Billowing clouds that bring no rain is the person who talks big but never produces" (MSG).

IT IS WISE TO UNDERSTATE AND OVER-PERFORM.

It's the difference between "walkers" and "talkers." As a leader, we do not need to say a lot when it comes to example. It is wise to understate and over-perform. When we do, people will willingly join arms with us on the journey; there will be no need to sound trumpets and hire crowds to announce our forthcoming initiatives. Our track record is all the advertising we will need. The Bible calls this "fruit" and says that we should be measured according to the quality of fruit being borne of our lives.[1]

A wise leader allows their fruit to speak for them; they do first and speak later, if necessary. Their critics are silenced by their results. Talkers make a lot of noise, overstate and underperform. They tend to be reactionary and opinionated, quick to identify problems, yet slow to take responsibility and action. Their talk does not match their walk.

The disparity between our walk and our talk is the gap that calls our leadership credibility into question; the greater the gap, the more pointed the question. It is comforting to know that leadership credibility is not a matter of perfection but integrity. When who you are in person lines up with who you appear to be from a distance, then this is the making of a great and worthy leader.

LEADERSHIP CREDIBILITY IS NOT A MATTER OF PERFECTION BUT INTEGRITY.

All the definitions of integrity simply mean that a person, substance or thing remains consistent in various conditions and under different forms of pressure.

PRESSURE CAUSES PERFORMANCE OR PUNCTURE, AND BOTH CAN BE CONSTRUCTIVE.

Remember that pressure is not always bad. Pressure causes performance or puncture, and both can be constructive. Obviously, performance is the most desirable outcome, but even if puncture takes place within a person's character or leadership ability, this can be utilised as a valuable learning opportunity for future growth.

As a general mantra for leadership, we need to be consistent with our values, our principles, our expectations of people and with the vision we are casting. Integrity and consistency are of utmost importance to the people you are *responsible over*. Talent (what people see in public) will earn you praise, but consistency (what is built in private) will earn you respect and followers.

Our culture celebrates a lot of great athletes and celebrities, but we would never follow most of them as life examples. Many of them do not hold the same values as we do, nor do they exemplify the way we might want to live our lives.

It is amazing how enamoured the world can be by celebrities, failing to see the inconsistency in their lives. Celebrities are asked to speak as experts on climate change while they fly private pollutant-omitting jets between environmental rallies. It is amusing and tragic that celebrities are looked up to for answers in the world.

Fame should never be a qualifier for leadership influence because celebrity status does not immediately qualify for credibility. In turn, we must remain mindful and vigilant for our own lives that "celebrity Christianity" does not infect our souls as we gain influence.

In life, you teach what you know, but you reproduce who you are. Much more is caught than taught. You can say a whole lot of impressive things, but at the end of the day, the proof of your leadership is shown in those

YOU TEACH WHAT YOU KNOW, BUT YOU REPRODUCE WHO YOU ARE.

around you who have picked up traits from who you are as a person. When we become who God wants us to be, we can reproduce who He wants for our generation.

Consistency produces its own fruit—good or bad. Therefore, it is important that our inner person is healthy. We will discuss this concept in greater depth in the last part of this book. For now, we will mention that who we are over the long term determines our example and is governed by who we are internally.

Keeping your inner world healthy will facilitate a healthy example. Do not become the thing you hate. Guard your heart because that is from where you live. When you do, others can judge you by your example, and when that is healthy, you will have a healthy team that follows.

DO NOT BECOME THE THING YOU HATE.

"Even so, every good tree bears good fruit, but a bad tree bears bad fruit. A good tree cannot bear bad fruit, nor can a bad tree bear good fruit. Every tree that does not bear good fruit is cut down and thrown into the fire. Therefore by their fruits you will know them."

(Matthew 7:17–20)

MAKE ROOM

KAROLINA GUNSSER

A leader will swing between the desire to have their team tight and right beside them while simultaneously desiring to release each one into a full and healthy expression of their potential.

While every leader would love to have a team of champions, many do not—because of the humbling task to lead those types of people.

Great leaders have teams full of people who are smarter and more capable than they are. If this statement were true, then we have to ask ourselves, "Why would someone of that calibre want to follow me?"

Unless we are narcissistic, we will admit that this is a confronting and challenging question. "What reasons am I giving this person to run alongside me?"

A GREAT LEADER WILL CREATE A PLATFORM, PROFILE AND SPOTLIGHT, THEN SHARE IT WILLINGLY WITH THOSE WHO ARE GREATER THAN THEM.

To have people on a team who exceed our abilities means that we have to create space for them. We have to welcome their diversity, their insight and their ideas. A great leader will create a platform, profile and spotlight, then share it willingly with those who are greater than them. This leader will be able to do this while maintaining their personal confidence as the leader of the team.

The sign of a true leader is if they can celebrate someone more skilled than themselves.

When we have giants on our teams, we know they will push us. Their capacity will stretch us. Their mindsets will challenge ours. They will set a new standard and norm within the whole team. When this stretch is created, a void appears that draws the rest upwards. We should expect our teams to be the best they can be and know that this causes us all to grow together.

It is easier to lead people just like us. It is easier to fall into our own defaults and run with people who "get us." It is also within our human nature to feel comfortable in a team that strokes our ego and agrees with every move we make. This attitude is opposite to the Kingdom culture and restricts legacy for future generations.

We should want to grow ourselves, and we should want to allow room for growth in those around us. It should be a genuine desire to be surrounded by mighty men and women who choose to join arms with us rather than blindly toeing the line.

This in no way condones obnoxious behaviour among team members. No matter how talented a person may be, no person should behave as though they are "God's gift." In military terms, a well-decorated soldier recognises and honours authority. A person who usurps authority displays immaturity and will create conflict within a team environment.

Often, the most influential people in our organisations are still waiting in the wings, observing and quietly supporting the cause. They are often not approached or invited for reasons such as intimidation or erroneous assumptions about their time or willingness.

They are high capacity potential team members, with hearts of gold and swift hands, but they remain outside the team because the leader does not know how to lead them.

Leading high-calibre people have practical ramifications; these types of people are aware of their own personal callings. They are living full lives and making an impact in the world. Therein lies the tension. Often, they may not be "too busy" to join our teams; they may just be waiting on a vision big enough to include them; and a leader confident enough to draw them in while maintaining an open and releasing hand.

LIFE IS RICHER WHEN LIVED WITH AN OPEN AND RELEASING HAND RATHER THAN A CLOSED AND CONTROLLING FIST.

Life is richer when lived with an open and releasing hand rather than a closed and controlling fist.

On the other hand, while a great leader will seek out great thinkers and people with developed skill sets, they will also commit to a life of creating this in others. To see the raw potential in someone and lead him or her boldly into his or her own greatness is a miraculous work in itself.

It sounds noble and inspiring, but what happens when they arrive? What happens when their wings are strong enough, and they are ready to soar into the wide blue yonder? What happens when our humanity wants to take credit for who they have become, and we want to clip their wings so they will stay close? Can we, at that moment, be the ones who flick on the neon sign that has their name up in lights? Can we celebrate their greatness, or does intimidation tighten our grip and close our fist? It takes a remarkable stoic heart to create and attract champions, then release them into their calling.

In Scripture, David attracted some of the rawest crew imaginable when he was exiled (by a King who could not lead or celebrate great men). These men were thugs and criminals who rallied around a quiet but strong David in the wilderness. He was not after position or title; he just invested heart and soul into the motley crew around him. They were later listed and named in 2 Samuel 23 as "David's Mighty Men."

These men were recorded for their many plights in defending God's people. They went from being social outcasts to heroes. Their names were recorded, and their deeds celebrated.

A team of giant slayers must be trained, believed in and released. David could conquer his quota of giants, but the synergistic effects of thirty other giant-slaying warriors were exactly what the nation needed, and David knew that.

The best leader will want to be outdone by those they are training. The big picture is greater than the role we each individually play. A great leader will toil and invest till they see their team meet their potential and will remind each one that the cause is what unites their individual callings.

CHAPTER 5:

IRRESISTIBLE ENVIRONMENTS

KAROLINA GUNSSER

Many leaders can sympathise with the frustration of dealing with a resistant team member, possibly even rebellious. Before we go ahead and label them as misguided mavericks, we as leaders should assess how much of their behaviour is reactionary and how much is intentional. Perhaps we have the ability to "win them over" if their behaviour is more reactionary than calculated intention.

So how do we draw a team member closer who is not "leaning in"?

As leaders, we are the thermostats for our teams. We must make the distinction between a thermometer, which reads the temperature, and a thermostat, which sets the temperature. As leaders, we

WE MUST MAKE THE DISTINCTION BETWEEN A THERMOMETER, WHICH READS THE TEMPERATURE, AND A THERMOSTAT, WHICH SETS THE TEMPERATURE.

create an atmosphere for our teams. When the atmosphere is attractive, we have created an environment where people *want* to lean in and be involved.

Much of the Kingdom of Heaven is about attraction. Jesus put it this way:

"But seek first the kingdom of God and His righteousness, and all these things shall be added to you."

(Matthew 6:33)

The principle of attraction holds especially true in a leadership context for building and leading teams. When the right elements are in place within a team, then the right people are attracted and grown within that environment.

We must constantly be asking ourselves the following questions:

» Why would anyone choose to be on my team?
» What is it about my team that a Kingdom-minded person would find irresistible?
» What is it about my team that could be repelling people?
» What is the atmosphere, temperature and culture of my team, and who is helping me set it?

In the following sections, we will explore some of the elements that contribute to creating irresistible environments.

EFFECTIVE COMMUNICATION

MARK RAMSEY

Communication and encouragement are vital to create irresistible environments. While nice thoughts about our team members are great, they hold limited power. We must communicate the value that each team member holds. We need to be good at regular feedback—both positive and negative.

Most parents find themselves coaching their children to "use their words" and communicate effectively. The same applies to leadership. Never assume someone knows how you feel about him or her. Never assume someone knows you value and appreciate him or her. "Use your words," and let them know through encouragement, edification, celebration and positive feedback. Seize the immediate moments to do this; do not delay if you can avoid it. As a leader, your words carry weight, and so, your encouragement and positive edification mean a lot to the members of your team.

When we communicate value, we validate the efforts of our team members. As leaders in this divine narrative, we cannot fall under the fallacy that tells us we do not pay volunteers. We actually do. We pay our teams in a currency that brings

THE CURRENCY WE PAY VOLUNTEERS WITH IS THE WORTHINESS OF THE CAUSE.

more joy and arouses more passion than any dollar amount. The currency we pay volunteers with is the worthiness of the cause. We help them realise that their investment is changing lives and making a difference.

Communicating the *why* behind the *what* is essential for ongoing team morale and passion. A good leader will continually let the team know *why* they do what they do. Even staff members who are paid financially need to be reminded regularly of the worthiness of their efforts. Small wins, as well as big wins, must be celebrated and communicated on the way towards the end goals.

Teams are compensated when their contribution to the cause is validated. You pay your team by validating the worthiness of the cause they are investing in. Communicating this clearly is the ultimate form of currency and reward for the team.

If you want to be a person others follow, you must be a good communicator. There are many forms of verbal and nonverbal communication; you do not have to be a preacher or professional public speaker to communicate effectively.

Communication brings clarity to the mission, unity of language and vibrancy to culture. Communication instils confidence because it allows everyone to be informed; it removes ambiguity and takes the guesswork out of play. Clarity is your friend when it comes to effective leadership.

Social media and technology have created so many avenues through which we can communicate. As leaders, we should seize these avenues as opportunities.

Leaders who have high expectations of others without communicating fairly and openly create havoc; they break trust and eventually lose followers and friends. We need to communicate clear expectations upfront, give fair feedback at the end and lavish a whole lot of encouragement and vision all the way along.

You must develop your communication skills and never cease developing them. Communicate the vision. Communicate the plan. Communicate expectations. Communicate gratitude. Communicate value. Above all things, you must continually communicate the worthiness of the cause. A leader will feel as though they are repeating themselves to no end, and yes, they probably are. However, a good leader understands that people are characteristically forgetful; life can quickly take the wind out of their sails and dull the shine of their dreams. Put simply, vision leaks.

Just when you feel like you have said it a thousand times and you can hardly bear the sound of your own voice saying it one more time, you can be almost certain that your team is just starting to catch what you have been communicating all that time.

WE OFTEN OVERSTATE WHAT CAN BE ACHIEVED IN TWELVE MONTHS AND UNDERESTIMATE WHAT IS ACHIEVED IN FIVE YEARS.

We often overstate what can be achieved in twelve months and underestimate what is achieved in five years. What we can achieve comes down to consistent and focused communication over a long period of time. It takes years to change and set culture, and effective communication is paramount to success.

We do not give up our time and energy and sow sacrificially just to feel good about ourselves or because we have nothing better to do with our time. No! We are here to change the world for Jesus Christ. Lives will be changed. People will be saved. There will be healing and deliverance. The cause is great, and our contribution is making a difference. Let your team know. Remind them often.

A person who values those they are *responsible over* makes a habit of celebrating the great cause the team is a part of and the collective wins achieved towards the goal. This leader understands and frequently communicates each team member's value in furthering the mission.

When we speak positively to and about another person, we are releasing the truths of Heaven over their life. That is what it means to bless a person—to activate Heaven's intention over their life. Our words and our deeds carry the power to unlock Heaven in people's lives. When we bless others in the way we communicate, we agree with what Heaven says about them. When we criticise, diminish or mock a person, we agree with the accuser. This is not a position any Christian leader should find themselves in.

WHEN WE SPEAK POSITIVELY TO AND ABOUT ANOTHER PERSON, WE ARE RELEASING THE TRUTHS OF HEAVEN OVER THEIR LIFE.

Whether this is by casting vision, blessing through encouragement or giving appreciation and celebration, our communication bears the most impact when it activates and releases Heaven on earth.

GENEROSITY

MARK RAMSEY

Great leaders are great givers.

We must understand that nothing leaves Heaven until something is given first on earth. Giving is a biblical principle and a spiritual law. Giving is what brings something from Heaven to earth. Six thousand years ago, Abraham gave his only son, and four thousand years later, God gave His only Son, Jesus.[1]

Jesus gave up His own life on earth to release salvation from Heaven for all humanity. Then Jesus said, "I must go so that He, the Holy Spirit, can come."[2] Faith must be given in prayer before miracles are released.[3] Tithes must be given to activate protection and blessing.[4]

Something always has to be given on earth before anything is released from Heaven. The principle of generosity is not just a nice idea; it is a spiritual weapon. This is precisely why the enemy fights so hard against it in an effort to bind up believers.

The measure of a leader is not the number of people who serve them but the number of people who they serve. Good leaders give of themselves and give themselves.

John Maxwell says, "A person must soon forget himself to be long remembered. He must empty himself in others to discover a fuller self. He must lose himself to find himself. Forget yourself into greatness."[5]

In other words, leadership is a selfless and generous life desiring to make a difference for others without needing to be recognised for it or applauded. Make sure that you are a generous leader. To take on the mantle of leadership is to assume and accept the greatest sacrifice.

SELF-SACRIFICE NOT SELF-PRESERVATION

KAROLINA GUNSSER

There is a significant difference between self-preservation and self-sacrifice. Our flesh wars against self-sacrifice. By human nature, we are primarily self-oriented creatures. Since generosity is a character trait of the Holy Spirit, it is the empowerment of the Holy Spirit that moves us into selfless living and Kingdom-minded leadership.

Generosity opens doors and has the power to change the order of things.[6] It is a leadership tool that is motivated from deep within. It cannot be manufactured or synthetic in nature. It is rooted in love and pure motives, with the interests of others at its core. Jesus told us, "Greater love has no one than this, than to lay down one's life for his friends" (John 15:13).

Self-preservation should never be the goal. Certainly, it was not the model given to us by Jesus or the early apostles and disciples. Just imagine if Jesus had chosen the life of self-preservation rather than self-sacrifice. The implications are simply unfathomable. The reason Jesus was the ultimate leader was that He displayed the greatest love ever expressed.

As leaders, we live our lives poured out. The Apostle Paul told his young disciple, Timothy, "Imitate me, just as I imitate Christ" (1 Corinthians 11:1 NLT). Paul gave of himself fully as he learned from the model given to him by Jesus. He was generous with his life, a replica of the life his Saviour had lived. In his example of living sacrificially, Paul wrote to the believers in Philippi, saying, "I am being poured out as a drink offering" (Philippians 2:17).

It would not be wrong to consider that graveyards might just be some of the wealthiest sites across the globe. Filled with books unwritten, songs unsung, inventions uncreated, potential unmet and dreams never realised. Living a generous life empties us of the Heaven deposited within us. It means we can "die empty," poured out, having run our race and having given our all.[7]

Could our obsession with accumulation and our tendency towards self-preservation be subtle temptations of the enemy to restrict God's full expression on earth through His sons and daughters? A selfless leader is a generous leader and one who becomes a conduit from Heaven to earth.

BEING GENEROUS IS THE SIGNATURE OF A BIG-THINKING PERSON.

Being generous is the signature of a big-thinking person. It is also evidence of wholeness and health. Generosity defies mentalities of entitlement and victimhood. It is a declaration to the world that "I have the capacity to contribute something of significance."

A leader who is generous to their teams sows sacrificially, practically, intentionally and regularly. In a world that says, "He who has the most wins," the Kingdom of Heaven says, "He who gives the most wins." Why is this so? Because, to quote our Saviour, "It is more blessed to give than to receive" (Acts 20:35).

Giving is likened throughout Scripture to sowing seed. The primary purpose of a healthy seed is to bear a harvest of fruit. When we sow generously, we can expect to see healthy growth. The Bible calls this a blessing.

While sowing is the beginning of a season, receiving is the end or close of a season. A wise person understands the exciting future prospect attached to every moment of generosity.

When we invest in our teams, we live by vision, and we anticipate growth. We place value on the soil of our teams, and we sow generously, remembering that every seed is designed to bear fruit. When we are motivated by the leadership responsibility and privilege of drawing the potential out of others, we give generously to see it come to pass.

Invest in the personal development of each member in the team you are *responsible over*. Be generous. And above all, do not grow weary in doing so because, in due season, those seeds will come to fruition.

And let us not grow weary while doing good, for in due season we shall reap if we do not lose heart.

(Galatians 6:9)

Of all the things we should be known for as Christian leaders, one of the most important things should be generosity. It is a character trait of the Holy Spirit, and therefore should be evidenced in the life and conduct of a Christian leader.

Having developed our understanding of leading those we are *responsible over*, it is time to break the myth that this dimension of leadership is the only or most significant way to lead. As we delve into the next three sections of this book, we will come to understand that there is indeed more than one way to lead, and all are required to expand our influence for us to become leaders of significant impact.

LEADING THOSE I AM RESPONSIBLE OVER

PERSONAL REFLECTION:

Empowerment
Do I have a tendency to use people or empower them?

Why is it important to be confident when inviting
someone to be involved in serving the vision?

Communication
What is the best way to communicate
clearly to my team?

Rewarding Team
How do I compensate the people on my team
beyond a monetary transaction?

How can I deepen this reward for my team?

Team
How do I inspire those who are highly skilled
to serve the vision?

PART TWO:

LEADING THOSE I AM
RESPONSIBLE WITH

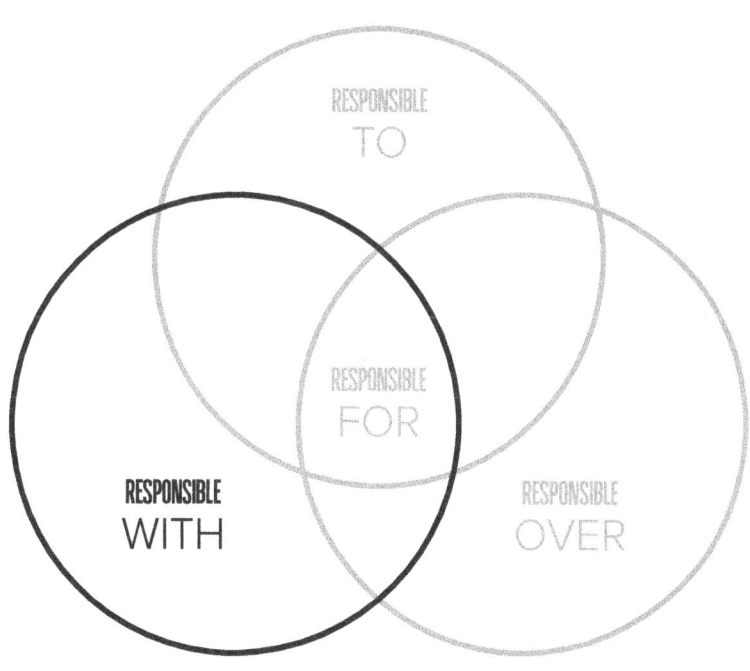

(PROVERBS 17:17)

A friend loves at all times,

And a brother is born for adversity.

"Friendship is unnecessary, like philosophy, like art, like the universe itself (for God did not need to create). It has no survival value; rather it is one of those things which give value to survival."

– C.S. LEWIS

CHAPTER 6:

LEADING THOSE BESIDE ME

MARK RAMSEY

The second view of leadership is one not spoken about often. Not only do we need to steward the teams we are *responsible over*, but we also need to lead those we are *responsible with*. These are our peers, our friends and our colleagues. Few people understand the powerful dynamic of leading those people on the same team standing on either side of them.

Not many realise that the interaction they have with peers, friends and colleagues is a function of leadership. It is one of the most powerful cultural forces within any organisation.

We lead our friends and colleagues by being valued team players, setting the example, setting culture, being servant-hearted and filling gaps. We lead our peers by celebrating each other's wins and supporting each other's needs.

I am reminded of the power of this every time our volunteer teams gather throughout the year. We call these gatherings "ONE Nights." Literally, hundreds of volunteers come together from all our locations in Brisbane, Australia, and celebrate victories, look towards the future and have a great time dressing up, theming their tables and eating the food they have all contributed. It's quite a sight. Dozens of round tables are decorated and catered by teams from different campuses across the city, all under one roof celebrating a common goal and each other. This is the quintessential snapshot of healthy peer leadership.

Truly effective leaders are not just people who effectively lead the teams they are *responsible over*, but they have worked out how to lead in the other three areas as well. Because they are an expanded leader, they have the capacity to take on greater roles and go to new levels.

This dimension of leadership is important to understand as it shows us that we can also lead the people beside us. The organisation always works better when everybody is moving in the same direction. This particular dimension of leadership values unity, celebration and strong culture upheld by the greater whole.

This leader carries a genuine interest in what other people do within the organisation. When the youth pastor is interested in what the administration team does, this brings a sense of relationship to the team that builds strength. We might have different oars, but we are all in the same boat, and we need to encourage each other all the way to the finish line.

WE MIGHT HAVE DIFFERENT OARS, BUT WE ARE ALL IN THE SAME BOAT.

CHAPTER 7:

ACTIVATING THE SILENT MAJORITY

MARK RAMSEY

We must understand the power we have among our peers to bring influence and leadership so that together we can have a major impact on our generation.

Well-respected Church analyst and friend Samuel Chand unlocked a powerful principle for our Church in more recent years. He identified three distinct groups within every organisation, whether it is corporate or religious in nature.[1]

The first 20 per cent of any organisation or people group are easily excited, on-board and ready to be involved with what is happening in the organisation. These are predominantly the people who make up leadership groups and volunteer teams. They are compelled and motivated.

Following them are 60 per cent of people who are not quite as excited or ready to action new things. They are not opposed; they are just not as quick to respond. This is the majority of your congregation or your customer base.

The remaining 20 per cent are those who will never really change; they are happy to keep things the same and rarely become excited about what is taking place. They can be passive, sceptical and even resistant to change. Even if you speak to this group in a visionary and direct manner, they still do not seem to hear or catch what is being cast.

The core of our teams is usually made up of the top 20 per cent. This information is relatively common knowledge, and it was not anything new to our Church leadership team. However, what we did learn came as refreshing enlightenment to help move us forward.

The key to cultural change and organisational growth actually lies in the hands of those 60 per cent of people in the second tier, whom Chand calls "mid adopters." These are the ones who are motivated and moved by the testimony and example of their peers.

For any organisation to lead in the marketplace, any Church to truly impact their world for Jesus, it has to effectively activate more of the 60 per cent to create a positive peer pressure in the right direction. The key is in how they do this.

Amazingly, the "mid adopters" in your congregation or organisation, who make up the majority, do not respond to the motivation given by the top tier of senior leaders.

In other words, a senior leader could preach his or her heart out and talk significantly about all that the organisation is going to do; they could do it week-in-week-out, year-in-year-out, and yet the majority of the organisation would not be moved into action.

Herein lies the significant aspect: although 60 per cent are not moved by top-down leadership, they are very much moved by the opinions and actions of their peers. For any organisation to move more of the 60 per cent into action, it will not be the senior leadership who influences them but rather their peers and those they are *responsible with*. More specifically, it comes from the peers within the top 20 per cent.

For many years, top-tier leaders have lived in a false sense of power, thinking that everything rests primarily on their direct influence when the reality is quite different. The silent majority made up of interacting team members have the power to shift whole organisations.

The move of God that will come into our generation will not come predominantly through pastors and senior leaders preaching and casting vision (though we will continue to do those things), but it will come when every person on the team understands the influence they hold in the lives of those they are working *with*.

Senior leaders must understand that the mobilisation of their organisation will not come through them alone; it is going to come through the team they lead carrying influence to those they are *responsible with* and the greater cohort of the organisation.

This is reflected powerfully in the model Jesus employed while He was here on the earth. He mobilised several tiers of peer groups and disseminated the message and the ministry through them; first with His closest three disciples, then the other nine disciples, and then the seventy (in some translations, seventy-two) followers.[2]

Jesus never intended to be the go-to-man for all ministry, encounters and revelation; He trained and mobilised teams to do "greater works" than even He would do.[3] So convinced was He about the power of an active majority that He even rebuked His disciples when they tried to restrict the work of some who were not directly connected to their immediate team.

> John said to Jesus, "Teacher, we saw someone using your name to cast out demons, but we told him to stop because he wasn't in our group."
>
> "Don't stop him!" Jesus said. "No one who performs a miracle in my name will soon be able to speak evil of me. Anyone who is not against us is for us."

(Mark 9:38–40 NLT)

Jesus was saying, "Friends, we should not control or limit this message to a small group of people. The more people sharing the good news and the miracle-working power of God, the better." Then, in His final address just before leaving the earth, He commissioned *all* followers, present and to come, not just leaders, for the work of the Kingdom.[4]

As leaders, we must place emphasis and authority back in the hands of every team member to move beyond personal excitement and revelation into influence. We must help them understand that it is their job to encourage and activate other people. They must move from being excited doers to encouragers, inspirers and vision casters. They must lead those they are *responsible with*.

THE MAJORITY OF PEOPLE ARE NOT IMPRESSED WITH TITLES AND POSITIONS; THEY ARE MOVED BY THE INFLUENCE OF THEIR PEERS.

If you are not in senior leadership, this is a significant dimension of leadership for you. Whether you have a leadership position or not makes very little difference when it comes to setting an example and acting consistently. The majority of people are not impressed with titles and positions; they are moved by the influence of their peers. They want to know that someone they can relate to is thinking bigger than they do right now, and they are willing to follow that person.

We must recognise how much power we hold to influence and bring change. We cannot be scared to ask somebody to step up and be involved with a great cause alongside us. We cannot be scared to sow into somebody's life and destiny, to encourage them to go further than they have before. Our colleagues and friends are the ones who hold weight with us in the Spirit realm to lead in such a way that more of Heaven comes to earth.

Every subsequent tier of leaders within an organisation must engage and invite others to join them on the journey. It sounds like discipleship, doesn't it? The good news is that the majority of people are going to respond positively. Inspiring those on either side of us has great synergistic power within an organisation to turn average into great.

A leader must ask their top 20 per cent not just to do things for the Kingdom of God but also to inspire others to join them in doing so. Team players, please recognise the power you hold to move your entire organisation into its future.

Our teams are often reminded of this principle when we hold events in our Church. Many people have testified over the years that a personal invitation to come along to an event was far more compelling than weeks of social media advertising and public announcements.

Recently, we heard from a lady who said that she came to one of our women's events because an intern sent her a personal text message inviting her to come. That lady sat in our services every week leading up to the event and heard the announcement given by senior leaders from the stage. After having decided that she would not attend, her mind was changed at the personal invitation of a friend.

In 2017, our nation went to a plebiscite on the definition of marriage. During the campaign season, I posted something on Facebook stating my position. To my surprise, there were over 90,000 views of it, which was more than expected, and only five death threats, which was less than I expected. In speaking with social media experts, they were not impressed that the post had 90,000 views. To the experts, the number of views was not the significant measurement but the fact that the post received 1,100 shares. They explained that it was the 1,100 shares that ultimately equated to the 90,000 views.

This exemplifies the power of harnessing an ability to lead those you are responsible with. If the 20 per cent are sharing the information, it drives into greater scope and influence. It was not just my post that was important; it was that 1,100 other people decided to get involved, which enabled the post to reach 90,000 people.

When a leader and their top 20 per cent understand the potential of their influence to motivate the greater majority of the organisation, they have tapped into a resource more powerful than the leader alone.

When leading those we are *responsible with*, we tap into a power to break barriers and defy the status quo in our organisations. This points to one question: "If I am to carry influence within my team and among my peers, how do I become a leader other people want to follow?" (John Maxwell).[5]

BE WORTH FOLLOWING

A team player must be clear about their mission if they want to see success. They have to know what they are a part of and their role within it. They have to know where they are heading personally and how their momentum contributes to the overall direction of the team as a whole. Even if it is not their own vision, perhaps the adopted vision cast by the senior leader, the team member still needs to have a strong sense of conviction and ownership of that vision.

The team player has to have a good idea of how they are going to arrive at the desired destination. There is no point in just saying, "We are going to change the world." Everyone wants to know how. We need to have some sort of plan or strategy.

Great leaders know they cannot achieve the mission alone. They look either side of themselves at those they are *responsible with* and work together. Some great leaders may know this instinctively; others will intentionally cultivate this dimension of leadership in their lives. They are not lone rangers; they value others and embrace peer level relationships.

In fact, people need leadership as much as they need friendship. They think they want friendship when what they really are searching for is someone who will help lead them into

PEOPLE NEED LEADERSHIP AS MUCH AS THEY NEED FRIENDSHIP.

their future. As friends and colleagues, we are endowed with the privilege of encouraging each other into the future.

Without leadership, a person may never reach their full potential. A leader's job is to inspire someone to do something they did not think they could do or to help them outwork a gift in their life that they did not know they had. As much as we need people to help us achieve organisational goals, those people also need us to speak into their lives to say to them, "You can. You've got this. You can win."

WITHOUT LEADERSHIP, A PERSON MAY NEVER REACH THEIR FULL POTENTIAL.

Our friends need us to speak into their lives confidently. It is important not just to become a star player but also to be a person others on the team want to work with and follow.

The Apostle Paul addressed this aspect of leadership in his first letter to his young disciple, Timothy.

> Let no one despise your youth, but be an example to the believers in word, in conduct, in love, in spirit, in faith, in purity.

> (1 Timothy 4:12)

Admittedly, this Scripture appeals to young leaders. As the more seasoned people remember the old days and humbly admit they no longer have anyone "despising" their youth, we can all admit a fundamental truth: we are called at all times to lead by example in every aspect of our lives. This has the power to influence those around us, especially our friends and colleagues.

COMPETITION SHARPENS THE EDGE

We want people to be competitive without having a spirit of competition, and there is a big difference. Being competitive motivates you to be the best you can be, while the spirit of competition will pull down others and revel in their demise to make oneself look and feel better.

You may have heard of a man named Brian Houston, the Global Senior Pastor of Hillsong Church. We are good friends, but we are competitive. I have at times spoken at his conferences, and he has at times spoken at ours. Not too long ago, I was invited to speak at Brian's Church conference as a part of a panel in one of the sessions. But earlier that same year, Hillsong had just started a new Church campus just five minutes down the road from one of our campuses.

Brian asked me, "What did you think of Hillsong Church starting down the road from you, Mark?" I'm not exactly sure what he thought I was going to say in response to that question. But I responded in front of a packed crowd, "I'll tell you what I tell everybody else—you want to be really good at what you are doing if Hillsong Church moves in next to you. The good news about Citipointe is that we are really good at what we do." Brian interjected and said, "Ramsey, I can't believe you put a Citipointe sign right out the front of the Hillsong campus." So if you go past Hillsong Church on that road in Brisbane, you will see a Citipointe sign pointing traffic in our direction.

In reality, it is local government councils that install those types of signs. However, as well as being humorous, the story paints a healthy case in point. The truth is that our cities all need as many thriving churches as possible. Competition is not the ugly brother of intimidation. Competition can be a healthy motivator that compels us individually and moves us forward.

Paul wrote about healthy competition in his first letter to the Church in Corinth.

> Do you not know that those who run in a race all run, but one receives the prize? Run in such a way that you may obtain it.

(1 Corinthians 9:24)

Herein lies the essential key: we are competitive, but we do not have a spirit of competition.

Competitiveness sharpens the edges and compels us to be the best we can be, but if it morphs into a spirit of competition, we will begin to see division, backbiting and an eventual unfolding of internal and external breakdown. We want our teams to be filled with people who are doing their best but not at the expense of others. Our desire to succeed should never pull others down to make oneself look or feel better.

Let us make sure we are the type of people who build one another up. Let us create team environments where we are all beating our own personal bests and celebrating each other along the way. When we influence those we are *responsible with* through inspiration, we have expanded our leadership capacity.

TAKE A GENUINE INTEREST

In his classic best-selling book, *How to Win Friends and Influence People*, Dale Carnegie communicates timeless truths about how to increase influence through self-awareness and exceptional people skills.[6] Much of leadership involves interaction with people, and success depends on the skills you possess to build rapport and trust. Leading those you are *responsible with* will require you to practice the art of verbal encouragement with fellow team members.

As mentioned in an earlier section, great leaders are generous with their praise, and they are not selective with the recipients of those words. They encourage those they are *responsible over*, *responsible with* and *responsible to*. They do not wait for the annual volunteers' event to nominate and applaud others; they consistently and frequently lavish encouragement walking down corridors and past offices.

Taking a genuine interest in what your colleagues are involved in will go a long way. Ask the questions, "How are you travelling? What have you got going on at the moment? What wins can I celebrate with you? What struggles can I help you with or pray for?" When you know what is happening in their world, you can then celebrate their successes and lend a hand in the struggles.

A GREAT LEADER ALWAYS ENCOURAGES PEOPLE.

A great leader always encourages people. When we do this, we are now leading the people around us by building strong relationships. Do not isolate yourself from the realities that your colleagues are facing. Look up from your post from time to time and take a genuine interest in what is happening around you. Connect with people on the issues that are of importance to them. This kind of person is on the fast track to expanded leadership.

We believe God not just for our own areas of responsibility within the organisation but for every other area to flourish as well. We are all in the same boat. We should be praying for the other departments to thrive and succeed. When we find ways to contribute to other people's goals, we unofficially take on more responsibility and achieve greater influence. In this process, we become bigger, stronger leaders.

In comparison, a small thinking and single-dimensional leader will only see what lies within the parameters of their own immediate job description. They assume anything outside of that scope is "not their department," and so they limit their involvement within the bigger picture.

What is interesting is that by isolating themselves, these types of people eventually feel like they have been pushed aside.

When in reality, they limited their involvement with others and their own relational reach. Often, they remain disconnected from others because they failed to become involved with the people alongside them.

In a congregational setting, this is similar to the faulty assumption that one can "find friends in Church." Our light-hearted response is often, "Well, have you looked under the chairs? That's where we keep them." People behave as though they expect to walk into a Sunday worship service and trip over a potential friend as they make their way down the aisle to their seat. The truth is, you do not *find* friends; you *make* friends.

So how do we *make* friends? We find ways to contribute to another person's efforts. We find ways to engage in matters that are important to the other person. In a team setting, we lend a hand to people on other teams, in other departments and working on other projects. We offer to help. We fill gaps. We look for needs and fill them. And when we do, we do not then brag or seek credit. We simply offer our involvement for the benefit of the relationship and the cause. We set others up to win.

People who effectively lead those they are *responsible with* do not wait to be encouraged; they give encouragement. They do not wait to be prayed for; they pray for others. They understand

WHEN ONE WINS, WE ALL WIN.

that when one wins, we all win, and so they make great efforts to influence the culture of the team towards this end through relational engagement, support, involvement and encouragement.

CHAPTER 8:

CELEBRATE

MARK RAMSEY

All leadership starts with an attitude. Not a bad attitude, but the right attitude—a balanced life is not about having a chip on both shoulders. The right attitude of a leader with their colleagues is one that is able to celebrate the success of the people around them.

They are able to say to their teammates, "Well done. Awesome job." They have an attitude that allows them to become excited when someone else on the team has a win and celebrate accordingly.

You do this by having an attitude that allows you to genuinely celebrate each other's success. It is a heartfelt and sincere motivation to highlight and praise somebody else. It is an understanding that someone else's success does not diminish my own; in fact, their success propels everyone else forward as well. When we understand that we are on the same team, we commit to seeing that every member succeeds, not just ourselves. This attitude brings strength to the overall team.

Right throughout history, we can observe a common phenomenon occurring in the demise of major civilisations. Societies began to fall from fractures within, from internal problems, not initially from external pressures. Eventually, opposing forces were able to take advantage of societies and organisations that were already compromised deep on the inside, making them weak and susceptible to attack from the outside.

It is not easy to defeat a strong enemy, but it is easy to defeat a weakened one. Learning from this teaches us the necessity for all team members to be guarding each other and celebrating each other regardless of departmental specifics or personal profiles and job descriptions. The overall strength of an organisation relies on each member within.

THE OVERALL STRENGTH OF AN ORGANISATION RELIES ON EACH MEMBER WITHIN.

A strong team does not only celebrate the few people in the spotlight; a strong team understands that the people in the spotlight are nothing without the ones turning the spotlight on and appropriately celebrating and valuing every member of the team. The unseen heroes need to be celebrated frequently.

This includes members of our grounds and facilities teams who do a near-impossible task. At the time of writing, our organisation runs several educational arms, including a school, higher education and ministry colleges and day care centres. Over fifty-two weeks each year, we run twenty-six weekly worship services in ten locations globally with 588 paid employees and over 1,816 volunteers. I'm well aware that it is the facilities and grounds staff that make a lot of what we do possible. We celebrate them publicly as often as we can, like we do with other seemingly "unseen" teams.

At each of our ONE Nights, we highlight and award a volunteer from each location. The truth is that everybody in the room is deserving of that award, but we cultivate a culture that celebrates the ones and twos highlighted at the moment, who then become healthy representatives of the collective whole.

By doing this, we recognise that when one wins, we all win. That is the spirit of somebody who can lead the people they are *responsible with*—their colleagues and friends. If we live like this, we defy and deny the negative spirit of competition. A quick and honest analysis soon discovers that many great organisations were not conquered first from the outside but from the inside. Even organisations that were eventually conquered from the outside, right throughout history, first became weak on the inside. Often this weakness is rooted in an unhealthy spirit of competition, jealousy or self-promotion.

The Bible speaks explicitly against the ways of envy and jealousy. God Himself laid down one of the Ten Commandments as a preventative measure against the disruptive practice of jealousy.[1] When departments and teams envy each other or speak badly of each other, we have a problem.

A good leader, however, understands that they not only lead the people they are *responsible over*, but they can also lead those they are *responsible with* by supporting and celebrating other teams within the organisation.

The Apostle Paul was seeking this type of support from the Church in Rome when he wrote to them saying that he wished to "be encouraged together" with them by their "mutual faith" (Romans 1:12).

This carries a sense of conviction that we can and should all win together. It starts with the right attitude, and then it is built and strengthened with action. You may be directly *responsible over* a handful of people, but you can have influence laterally with many more by doing a few simple things.

THE MIRACLES IN ONE ANOTHER

KAROLINA GUNSSER

Let us draw our attention to the account of the Virgin Mary—mother of our Saviour, Jesus. You may know the story of the angelic visitation she encountered as a teenage girl.

"Greetings highly favoured one! You are going to have a son," the angel announced to her. "You are going to call Him Jesus, and He will bring salvation to all mankind."[2]

Talk about a bombshell! Mary found herself in quite a predicament. She was unmarried and pregnant. I can just imagine her relaying this information to her fiancé, Joseph. "Joseph, I'm pregnant, and God is the father."

Not only was Joseph meant to believe Mary, but her entire community and family were presented with the same opportunity to assess the validity of her claims as well.

During this immensely difficult season, Mary set a significant example for us by visiting her friend and cousin, Elizabeth. The account is found in the first chapter of Luke's gospel.

> Now Mary arose in those days and went into the hill country with haste, to a city of Judah, and entered the house of Zacharias and greeted Elizabeth. And it happened, when Elizabeth heard the greeting of Mary, that the babe leaped in her womb; and Elizabeth was filled with the Holy Spirit.
>
> (Luke 1:39–41)

We have to remember that Elizabeth was also miraculously pregnant. An angel had visited Elizabeth and Zachariah just several months prior. He had prophesied to them they were going to have a son in their old age. Elizabeth, too, was carrying a miracle.

> Then she spoke out with a loud voice and said, "Blessed are you among women, and blessed is the fruit of your womb! But why is this granted to me, that the mother of my Lord should come to me? For indeed, as soon as the voice of your greeting sounded in my ears, the babe leaped in my womb for joy. Blessed is she who believed, for there will be a fulfilment of those things which were told her from the Lord."

> (Luke 1:42–45)

We learn a great deal from this exchange between Mary and Elizabeth. Leading those at a peer level requires that we are friends like Elizabeth was to Mary. We have come to call them Kingdom comrades.

A Kingdom comrade has the genuine ability to celebrate their friends. It is interesting that Mary went to Elizabeth in her first trimester. The Word of God on the inside of Mary was in its most fragile and most vulnerable stages. Mary carefully chose where she would spend that vulnerable season. She went to the safest place she could go and, on her arrival, was greeted enthusiastically by a woman who was carrying a miracle of her own.

These two expectant mothers resonated with each other. Kingdom comrades resonate with their friends at a deep level; they go beyond the superficial and celebrate the miracle at

KINGDOM COMRADES RESONATE WITH THEIR FRIENDS AT A DEEP LEVEL.

work within each other. When God is at work within their friends, Kingdom comrades arise with a genuine and authentic celebration over the miracle that is taking place for their friend.

Paul urged those in the Church of Philippi to value each other significantly beyond the effects of jealousy.

> Do nothing from selfish ambition or conceit, but in humility count others more significant than yourselves.

> (Philippians 2:3 ESV)

To be Kingdom comrades, we need to celebrate others. In order to do that sincerely, we must consider others as greater than ourselves. The greatest enemy of our ability to celebrate is jealousy. Jealousy may very well be the opposite of celebration.

When the Apostle Paul wrote to the brand-new Church in Corinth, he stated blatantly that their previous worldly nature still shows through in their jealousy of each other.

> ...for you are still controlled by your sinful nature. You are jealous of one another and quarrel with each other. Doesn't that prove you are controlled by your sinful nature? Aren't you living like people of the world?

> (1 Corinthians 3:3 NLT)

Jealousy stops your ability to lead people beside you. Jealousy is a trademark of worldly culture. We are called to be different from the world. We are called to love genuinely and authentically and to put others before ourselves. We are called to celebrate the goodness of God in each other.

Jealousy says, "What I have is not as good as what you have." Jealousy says, "What God has given me is not as significant as what God has given you." But celebration understands that God is moving in all of us. Celebration understands when one wins, we all win.

CELEBRATING ANOTHER PERSON'S WONDER WILL NOT DIMINISH OUR OWN.

We need to believe that celebrating another person's wonder will not diminish our own. Celebrating what God is doing in someone else does not diminish what He is doing in you. But if you can't see what God is doing in you, you will be jealous of what He is doing in someone else. Elizabeth was so aware of how blessed she had been that she could see and celebrate how blessed Mary was as well.

We need to be bigger people, not ones who are jealous when someone else is being celebrated. In fact, we should be the ones leading the celebratory parade.

> "Your love for one another will prove to the world that you are my disciples."

(John 13:35 NLT)

The love that we have for each other becomes a witness to the world, and it shifts atmospheres to successfully set a can-do culture. This has become one of the criteria we employ in our selection process when hiring staff or allocating volunteer positions. We want to see evidence of the candidate's ability to celebrate and lift the spirits of those around them. If they can do that and fulfil the practical requirements of the role, then things are looking promising for the candidate, their team and the mission.

The world is hurting and looking for answers, and they should be able to look to the Church and find those answers. In a "me first" consumerist culture, the Church should shine brightly as a people group who puts others before themselves and genuinely loves them.

A Kingdom comrade celebrates what God is doing in others and puts a generous voice to it. Properly leading those you are *responsible with* creates an environment that nurtures Heaven's deposit and intention within every member of the team. It joins arms with and agrees with the Holy Spirit, in turn, making room for personal growth in our friends, colleagues and peers.

SHARE THE BURDEN OF FAITH
KAROLINA GUNSSER

In Luke 8, we see our Saviour choosing who His peers will be for a challenging situation. It is the story of Jairus' daughter, who was pronounced dead. When Jesus arrived at the house, He had all His disciples with Him and a large crowd with them—there was always a crowd wherever Jesus went. By the time Jesus arrived at the house, another crowd was there, with everyone being caught up in a heightened state of hysteria.

> When they arrived at the house, Jesus wouldn't let anyone go in with him except Peter, John, James, and the little girl's father and mother. The house was filled with people weeping and wailing, but he said, "Stop the weeping! She isn't dead; she's only asleep."
>
> But the crowd laughed at him because they all knew she had died.

(Luke 8:51–53 NLT)

SOMETIMES THE EVENTS OF OUR LIVES WILL CALL US TO EXPEL CERTAIN GROUPS OF PEOPLE THAT WE DO NOT NEED AROUND.

Often, we find the crowd in our life can be quite fickle and sometimes insincere. We can see here that at one minute, the crowd is crying, and the next minute they are laughing at Jesus and mocking Him. Obviously, there are just some people that we need to kick out of the "house of our lives" on certain occasions. Sometimes the events of our lives will call us to expel certain groups of people that we do not need around.

> Then Jesus took her by the hand and said in a loud voice, "My child, get up!" And at that moment her life returned, and she immediately stood up! Then Jesus told them to give her something to eat. Her parents were overwhelmed, but Jesus insisted that they not tell anyone what had happened.

(Luke 8:54–56 NLT)

Jesus expelled a whole bunch of people from the vicinity of the situation. Interestingly, He turned to His twelve disciples and asked nine of them to remain outside.

This should make any person pause and wonder, who were the three that Jesus drew close? Who was it that met Jesus' criteria to stay in the room with Him? It was Peter, James and John.

Well, if you know anything about those three, you will know that they were the most irrational, illogical, politically incorrect, emotional, passionate and impulsive disciples out of the twelve.[3] And they are who Jesus wanted in the room. On examining the nine that were excluded, we find some were cynical, sceptical, self-orientated, analytical, agenda-driven or doubtful. Some people are just too smart for their own good, forever rationalising their way out of a miracle. It would seem that some people know too much to believe.

Jesus wanted Peter, James and John in the room. Reflecting on this begs the question of us quite directly: "Would I have been one of the three invited to stay in the room, or would I have been among the ones left outside the door?"

Would I be one of the three, or would I be one of the nine?

Peter, James and John were fully persuaded, emotionally invested men, and Jesus wanted them in the room when the miracle had to take place. When it came to ushering in a miracle, Jesus was selective about who He would lead alongside.

Are you that kind of person for your peers? Are you the one called into a room of faith? Effectively leading those we are *responsible with* allows us to facilitate the miraculous plans and purposes of God. An expanded leader is the kind of person who stands side by side with other teammates, in bold faith, believing together for the impossible.

This dimension of leadership expands our influence as colleagues and friends. Sharing the burden of faith invites us into rooms where great things take place.

CHAPTER 9:

STEPPING OUT
FROM THE CROWD

KAROLINA GUNSSER

There will potentially be times when a leader may have to address bad culture among peers and even close friends on the team. There may be other times that require a leader to step out from the pack, where a greater level of faith is required for the task at hand.

When the call to step out arises, we must remain vigilant in our motives and our conduct. We do not act from a self-righteous, "holier-than-thou" type attitude. We do this knowing that single acts of faith and obedience have the potential to bring the whole team forward. Sometimes the majority may dilute or compromise the plans and purposes of God. At those times, an act of boldness from even just one member of the team can benefit the greater whole.

Samuel urged Saul at his inauguration to be the kind of leader who would not fail to step up when the situation demanded a greater level of faith.

> "And let it be, when these signs come to you, that you do as the occasion demands; for God is with you."

> (1 Samuel 10:7)

Following are three hard truths that every wise peer leader should recognise when a time to step up is required. Let us explore them together.

CONFRONT BAD CULTURE

KAROLINA GUNSSER

In the first book of Samuel, we see David and his band of misfits living in exile and running from their leader, King Saul, who had quite seriously fallen into madness and become an obsessive, jealous and narcissistic leader. David did not officially hold the position of leader among these exiled men. He was a reluctant leader being followed by a group of the most dysfunctional social outcasts you could imagine. The one thing that united them all was the exile imposed on them by King Saul.

In 1 Samuel 26, we find these men camped once again dangerously close to Saul's army who were unaware of the proximity of these ones they were indeed pursuing. It would seem on this occasion that God had delivered Saul into the very hands of David.

> So David and Abishai entered the encampment by night, and there he was—Saul, stretched out asleep at the centre of the camp, his spear stuck in the ground near his head, with Abner and the troops sound asleep on all sides.
>
> Abishai said, "This is the moment! God has put your enemy in your grasp. Let me nail him to the ground with

his spear. One hit will do it, believe me; I won't need a second!"

But David said to Abishai, "Don't you dare hurt him! Who could lay a hand on God's anointed and even think of getting away with it?"

He went on, "As God lives, either God will strike him, or his time will come and he'll die in bed, or he'll fall in battle, but God forbid that I should lay a finger on God's anointed. Now, grab the spear at his head and the water jug and let's get out of here."

(1 Samuel 26:7–11 MSG)

David had an uncanny ability to uphold and impart Kingdom culture into those around him. He humbly, yet boldly, confronted and corrected poor culture among his friends. As a result of his conviction and resulting leadership, those outcasts and misfits who rallied around David became what we now know as "David's Mighty Men."[1]

We see from this passage in Scripture that God honoured David. Even Saul, in a moment of lucid revelation, was convicted by the integrity of David's actions.

IF THERE WAS EVER A TIME FOR GODLY LEADERS TO STAND IN THE FACE OF OPPOSING CULTURE, IT IS NOW.

Upholding the culture of Heaven is not always easy, fashionable or popular, but it is always right. There may, from time to time, arise a situation where we arrive at a crossroad—to either set Kingdom culture or buckle beneath compromise. Sometimes the pressure of peer opinion may seem great, and we may be outnumbered or even completely alone. It is in those times when our true resolve is being tested. If there was ever a time for godly leaders to stand in the face of opposing culture, it is now.

We must soberly ask ourselves if we are living for the acceptance of the majority or if we are living to honour and glorify God.

WE MUST SOBERLY ASK OURSELVES IF WE ARE LIVING FOR THE ACCEPTANCE OF THE MAJORITY OR IF WE ARE LIVING TO HONOUR AND GLORIFY GOD.

Regardless of which dimension of leadership we discuss throughout this book, the foundational motive should be this and this alone—to live for God. May we see greater and growing ranks of godly men and women in all spheres of influence, who care only for what the Father says about them. Our reputations in Heaven are of superior importance and always supersede the opinion of men. Often, leading those beside us and those we are *responsible with* demands that we rise up to set Kingdom culture among our friends and teams.

CARRY CONVICTION

KAROLINA GUNSSER

Not all team members carry an equal level of conviction or faith, for that matter. In testing times, this disparity can become glaringly obvious, and tensions can arise between peers and friends.

We see this in the account of the twelve spies who were sent to scout out Canaan in the book of Numbers. All twelve spies were on team with the same hierarchical position, the same mission, function and responsibility. However, upon completion of the mission, ten of the twelve gave opposing reports to those of Caleb and Joshua.

> "We went to the land to which you sent us and, oh! It does flow with milk and honey! Just look at this fruit! The only thing is that the people who live there are fierce, their cities are huge and well fortified. Worse yet, we saw descendants of the giant Anak. Amalekites are spread out in the Negev; Hittites, Jebusites, and Amorites hold the hill country; and the Canaanites are established on the Mediterranean Sea and along the Jordan."
>
> Caleb interrupted, called for silence before Moses and said, "Let's go up and take the land—now. We can do it."

> But the others said, "We can't attack those people; they're way stronger than we are." They spread scary rumours among the People of Israel.
>
> (Numbers 13:27–33 MSG)

Ultimately, ten spies influenced such fear and discord among the nation of Israel that the people became afraid to go into the land, which God had promised would be theirs. Caleb and Joshua insisted all along that God would go before them as a nation, and they should act in obedience and faith. Their voice of faith was drowned out by the masses, God was displeased, and an entire generation missed out on the blessing and promise.

In the very next chapter, we see God's perspective of the whole scenario. Pay close attention to the Lord's character reference for this man Caleb.

> Just then the bright Glory of God appeared at the Tent of Meeting. Every Israelite saw it. God said to Moses, "How long will these people treat me like dirt? How long refuse to trust me? And with all these signs I've done among them! I've had enough—I'm going to hit them with a plague and kill them. But I'll make you into a nation bigger and stronger than they ever were...."
>
> God said, "I forgive them.... But as I live and as the Glory of God fills the whole Earth—not a single person of those who saw my Glory, saw the miracle signs I did in Egypt and the wilderness, and who have tested me over and over and over again, turning a deaf ear to me—not one of them will set eyes on the land I so solemnly promised to their ancestors. No one who has treated me with such repeated contempt will see it.
>
> But my servant Caleb—this is a different story. He has a different spirit; he follows me passionately. I'll bring him into the land that he scouted and his children will inherit it."
>
> (Numbers 14:10–12, 20–24 MSG)

Immediately following this account, Moses, Aaron and the leaders spent four decades resolving strife and rebellion as the nation wandered aimlessly in the wilderness. Caleb and Joshua faithfully served Moses and Aaron until the time when they were appointed as the new leaders of Israel. Of the twelve spies who originally went into Canaan, Caleb and Joshua were the only ones to inherit the promise and lead the nation into the Promised Land.

Because of Caleb and Joshua's willingness to step out from the crowd, to rise above doubt and fear, to pursue the plan of God regardless of what their colleagues were saying and believing, Caleb and Joshua fulfilled the plan of God in their lifetimes and led the nation along with them.

THE VOICE OF FAITH WILL, ON OCCASION, CALL US TO RISE ABOVE WHAT THE MAJORITY BELIEVES.

There is always a lot at stake. The voice of faith will, on occasion, call us to rise above what the majority believes. Sometimes leading those we are *responsible with* may just look like this.

There is an old adage that says if we want to soar with eagles, we must be willing to stop scratching around with chooks.

> **"BE WHO YOU ARE AND SAY WHAT YOU FEEL, BECAUSE THOSE WHO MIND DON'T MATTER AND THOSE WHO MATTER DON'T MIND."**
>
> (ANONYMOUS)

OFTEN, LEADERSHIP REQUIRES STEPPING OUT FROM THE CROWD.

Often, leadership requires stepping out from the crowd.

A leader is never satisfied babysitting the status quo, especially when the great call and promise of Heaven is beckoning us to go deeper, further and greater. A person who leads those they are *responsible with* is one who lives by conviction and draws others upwards as they move in that direction.

The Apostle Paul told his followers to press ever upwards towards the call in Christ Jesus and to imitate him as he imitated Christ.[2] We are called to imitate Jesus alone and set Kingdom standards for our fellow team members as we do.

DO WHAT THE MASSES ARE AVOIDING

MARK RAMSEY

Greatness is always on the other side of inconvenience. Greatness does what everyone else is trying to avoid.

GREATNESS IS ALWAYS ON THE OTHER SIDE OF INCONVENIENCE.

We should do our best to avoid the mindset that immediately associates problems with pain. We should discipline our minds to believe that problems can, in fact, be pathways to opportunity. Pain or difficulty may ensue as we tackle what stands before us, but this should never be an excuse not to act.

Opportunity often dresses like a giant. The bigger the target is, the harder it is to miss.

OPPORTUNITY OFTEN DRESSES LIKE A GIANT.

Thomas Edison, the inventor of the light bulb, is said to have failed thousands of times. However, he redefined every so-called failure to be a lesson on how not to create light. It is to Edison we credit the saying, "Opportunity is missed by most people because it is dressed in overalls and looks like hard work."[3]

The greatest successes we will ever achieve will not arise because we overcame a small thing. Successes eventuate because we succeed at something; we succeed because we overcome, and overcoming by its very nature requires the mastery of a difficult thing. Solving problems is the nature of growth and victory.

To be the conqueror requires that we conquer something.[4] To be an overcomer implies that we have overcome.[5]

Scripture abounds with such examples.

David addressed the giant everyone else was hiding from. His sense of urgency and indignation and knowing God's plan compelled him to stand before the King to demand an opportunity to deliver the people; it enabled him to do what everyone else was avoiding and, in turn, he became a great leader of his peers. He led everyone around him without even having a title or position.

Even his own brothers tried to remind him of his lack of stature.[6] Regardless, David went ahead solving a problem no one else wanted to solve. As a result, the whole nation quite literally sang his praises and wrote chants in his honour.[7]

Joseph also solved problems everywhere he ended up. Most of the settings he found himself in were unfortunate and inflicted unfairly on him by the decisions and mistreatment of others.[8] Yet, he rose up every time and made the most of every situation. This gained him favour and promotion time after time after time.

Jesus was the greatest leader of all time because He solved the most significant problem to ever face humanity. He put His own life on the line for the sake of mankind. He made right the most grievous of all eternal dilemmas and offered salvation and deliverance to all.[9]

There is an old tale of a chicken farmer who lived in a small farming community prone to flooding. He came into financial hardship as a result of his chickens dying each time floodwaters rose. His land was undesirable for sale since nobody wanted to own a farm susceptible to seasonal flooding. One afternoon, while the despondent farmer was having a cup of tea with his wife, he voiced his frustration: "I don't know how to get us out of this situation." To which his wife replied, "Well if the chickens keep drowning, why don't we farm ducks?"

LEADERSHIP IS ABOUT HAVING THE CREATIVITY REQUIRED TO SOLVE PROBLEMS.

Put simply, leadership is not about just seeing problems. Almost anyone can do that. Leadership is about having the creativity required to solve problems. Creativity is not limited to the arts (more on this in the next section). Every leader has an innate creative ability to strategise, see a way forward and build something out of nothing.

Too many people have the mentality of trying to explain why they are in a certain situation rather than creating ways to get out. Quite often, it only takes one person to rise up with a solution and lead the whole group into breakthrough. Leadership is all about the creativity required to move forward into the next place God has for us.

If we want to be the sort of leaders other people want to follow, we can't be problem makers or problem seers; we need to be problem solvers. Rise up and do what the masses are avoiding.

Dream big dreams and use creativity to transform every challenge into an opportunity.

In the fifth grade, Walt Disney drew a flower garden. His teacher looked at his drawing and said, "Walt, that's not right. Flowers don't have faces on them." The young boy replied, "Excuse me, Ma'am, but mine do."[10] And to this very day, at every Disneyland theme park all over the world, every flower has a smiling face on it. Do not be afraid of creating new ways forward.

Our influence with fellow team members is arguably the most vigorous in the creation or reshaping of organisational culture. The dynamics between team members directly affect overall results. It goes without saying that these influences can be either for the betterment or detriment of the team's success.

THE DYNAMICS BETWEEN TEAM MEMBERS DIRECTLY AFFECT OVERALL RESULTS.

Developing the skill set required to lead in this dimension cannot be overstated. As we lay down self-centred agendas and promote others before ourselves, we propagate an ethos in which everyone wins. As we tune our ear to the call of Heaven, we silence fear and rise up in faith.

There is more than one dimension to leadership. Leading those we are *responsible with* is powerful and effective. Let us now expand our understanding of leadership into a third dimension. How is it possible to lead those you are *responsible to*—your leaders?

LEADING THOSE I AM RESPONSIBLE WITH

PERSONAL REFLECTION:

Silent Majority
Why is it important to give key leaders
a voice to mobilise the masses?

What are some practical ways I can do this
more effectively in my team?

Honour
Why is honouring not just those who are leading me,
but those who I am leading with, so important?

Jealousy
How can I avoid traps of jealousy and insecurity
when a peer is promoted?

Confronting Bad Culture
What is the best way to correct bad culture?

PART THREE:

LEADING THOSE I AM
RESPONSIBLE TO

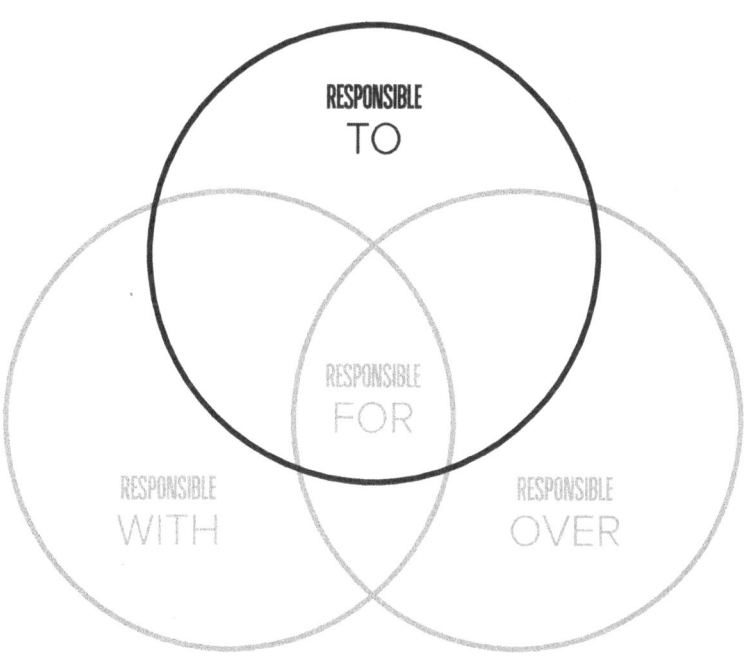

(HEBREWS 13:17 ᵀᴾᵀ)

Obey your spiritual leaders and recognise their authority, for they keep watch over your soul without resting since they will have to give an account to God for their work. So it will benefit you when you make their work a pleasure and not a heavy burden.

"When I was a boy of 14, my father was so ignorant I could hardly stand to have the old man around. But when I got to be 21, I was astonished at how much the old man had learned in seven years."

— **MARK TWAIN**

CHAPTER 10:

LEADING UP

MARK RAMSEY

The third context of leadership is with those you are *responsible to*—this dimension is underrated, but it is very powerful. This dimension of leadership requires an ability to recognise the influence we may carry to our "up-lines" and authorities, such as employers, teachers, leaders, civic authorities, parents and the like.

This third dimension of leadership may come as a surprise to some, but we can confidently say that it is possible to lead our leaders. While we can be *responsible over* the teams in our care, and we can have influence *with* those on the team beside us, there is quite an art to leading the leader.

We lead those we are *responsible to* by performing well, going above and beyond, taking initiative and releasing our leaders to run faster, not by slowing them down.

Understanding this dimension of leadership recognises that we can actually carry influence into the worlds of the leaders we serve. We can speak into their hearts and minds if we do it the right way.

Obviously, there are two sides to this coin. As the senior leader, it is important to understand that you do not have all the answers. As the follower, it is important to know that although you may have an answer, your approach can either create change or slam doors shut before you.

In this section, we will explore this dynamic relationship from both sides of the proverbial coin.

THE SENIOR LEADER: BEING LED BY YOUR FOLLOWERS

One of the great strengths of a good senior leader is the ability to seek and celebrate the opinions of others. We explored this dimension of leadership in the first section of this book; however, it is important to highlight it briefly here again. Some dynamic senior leaders have cultivated the humility required to allow them to be led by those they are leading.

Every senior leader must honestly evaluate what they "bring to the table." This requires a firm and sober grasp on what gift sets they contribute to the team and, just as importantly, what shortcomings they may have.

If you are a senior leader, what are your strengths, and what are your weaknesses?

Once this is established in the conscious mind of a senior leader, they can go about surrounding themselves with people who complement those strengths, as well as staff their areas of weaknesses. Through intentional design, they can craft a team of people who are smarter, more talented and exceeding in certain areas. We find here a secure senior leader who now has a well-formed, balanced team.

The next step is the true test. The senior leader must now allow those team members to speak into their decision-making processes. Smart leaders do not need to have all the right information; they just need to know where to find the right information. It has been said that an average leader assumes they have all the answers; an excellent leader asks great questions.

> **AN AVERAGE LEADER ASSUMES THEY HAVE ALL THE ANSWERS; AN EXCELLENT LEADER ASKS GREAT QUESTIONS.**

THE FOLLOWER: LEADING YOUR LEADER

We can actually lead our leaders without being a pain. It is entirely possible for our leaders to enjoy hearing our contributions, to enjoy resourcing our efforts and to celebrate the influence we carry in the organisation.

It is important to know we can bring about positive change and influence to our leaders. We can do this without being a traitor or starting a mutiny. Influencing effectual positive change never happens in secret hallway conversations about how bad things are. It is not about whingeing, complaining or nursing a belief that you could "do it better."

The ability to lead those we are *responsible to* begins and ends with trust. We must earn the right to be heard and trusted by our senior leaders. We see an example of this in the relationship between Moses and his father-in-law, Jethro.

> "Moreover you shall select from all the people able men, such as fear God, men of truth, hating covetousness; and place such over them to be rulers of thousands, rulers of hundreds, rulers of fifties, and rulers of tens. And let them judge the people at all times. Then it will be that every great matter they shall bring to you, but every small matter they themselves shall judge. So it will be easier for

you, for they will bear the burden with you. If you do this thing, and God so commands you, then you will be able to endure, and all this people will also go to their place in peace."

So Moses heeded the voice of his father-in-law and did all that he had said.

(Exodus 18:21–24)

In this passage, we see Moses, the leader of the nation, heeding the word of his father-in-law, Jethro. In his role as senior leader, Moses was facing the challenge of personal unsustainability. Recognising the restrictions of their limitations is vital to the future growth and expansion of the senior leader's influence and the ongoing impact of the organisation as a whole.

While Jethro carried no functional authority in Moses' civil ranks of advisors, he did carry significant relational influence with Israel's tired leader. He brought Moses a solution and a strategic plan. Jethro led his leader, Moses.

What takes place in order for this type of influence to transpire? In the next chapter, we will explore further what it means to lead our leaders—this time from the position of what we will come to know as the position of "the second."

CHAPTER 11:

THE POWER OF SECOND

KAROLINA GUNSSER

It is far too easy, almost human nature, for our attention to fall on the man or woman out the front. Often unseen are the ones immediately behind or beside, who assist in making the leader more effective.

Consider for a moment the likes of Silas and his role in Peter and Paul's ministries to the new Church. More than a mere companion, Silas was the scribe who penned the timeless words found in New Testament letters to the first churches and leadership teams. We often say that Paul wrote the majority of the New Testament, but it was by Silas' hand.[1]

We see it in Aaron with Moses, Caleb with Joshua, Ruth with Naomi and many others throughout both Scripture and the records of history. These mighty leaders had mighty men and women who understood their role beside the leader. No great leader can achieve any significant exploits on their own.

This section is dedicated to the ones who would consider themselves "a second." Your role is significant. Your role requires a deep revelation, deep humility and deep security in knowing exactly what it is that you bring to the overall cause that you are working towards.

Being a second in many ways holds a unique and spiritual gift set. There are cases in abundance that cite a second who may have at one point tried their hand at leading, only to come back into their sweet spot as a second.

The old adage that says, "There is no limit to what we can achieve if we care little for who gets the glory," rings true when it comes to leading those we are *responsible to* and being a second. All the mighty men and women of Scripture and throughout history can ascribe much of their success to the ones around them who were committed to the cause.

A commitment on your part is required for the chemistry between you and your leader to be effective and dynamic. It is a commitment that your leader cannot enforce or demand of you. The submission and honour necessitated in this role stem from revelation and a voluntary commitment that you make—you and you alone.

Submission, honour, obedience and compliance are not the same. The latter two can potentially be enforced, demanded even, as they merely require the appropriate outward behaviour to be exhibited. Submission, however, speaks to the posture of the heart, and true honour flows from the purity of revelation— understanding God's ordained blessing on the order that comes through proper channels of leadership.

Perhaps there is no greater illustration of this concept than John the Baptist. A man who was completely secure in who he was and who he was not. John understood his role as a forerunner, path blazer and signpost pointing to the Saviour.

I KNOW WHO I AM AND WHO I AM NOT.

When John's followers started deflecting their allegiances to follow Jesus instead of John, some sought to find out how he felt about his dwindling fame. His response was clear. "I know who I am and who I am not" was the basis of his answer.

> So John's disciples came to him and said, "Rabbi, the man you met on the other side of the Jordan River, the one you identified as the Messiah, is also baptising people. And everybody is going to him instead of coming to us."
>
> John replied, "No one can receive anything unless God gives it from heaven. You yourselves know how plainly I told you, 'I am not the Messiah. I am only here to prepare the way for him.'"

(John 3:26–28 NLT)

Understanding the role he was to play in the grand scheme allowed him to resist impulsive reactions, jealousy, intimidation and the broad gamut of responses that are rooted in insecurity and pride.

More powerfully perhaps is the soberness and self-awareness John possessed, which allowed him to accurately measure the success of his ministry. While we are in no way suggesting any earthly leadership replicates the status of our Saviour, we have much to glean from John's understanding of the power of second.

What better privilege is there than to play a part of something greater than you could ever achieve on your own!

LEARNING TO BE A "SON"

A common term in culture over recent years has been in reference to a "fatherless generation." This term has stemmed from the unfortunate breakdown of the family unit in our day. The result has become a family home where fathers are often not present or engaged with their children.

While there has been a fair share of social commentary around this reality and fathers have received their dose of scolding and judgement, there is a secondary phenomenon that is rarely noted or observed; we now have a generation of sons and daughters who don't know how to be sons and daughters.

Resulting from the absenteeism of fathers is a rising generation who do not know how to honour, learn from and interact with the older generation. When we consider that the most foundational concept of Kingdom identity we have is as sons and daughters of God, this presents significant challenges in the Kingdom of Heaven for our generation.[2]

Studying Scripture highlights a powerful truth for us as spiritual sons and daughters of those in authority over us. Under close examination, we find that a great deal of the onus falls on the "sons" when learning how to appropriately interact in this relationship. Two of the most pointed examples we have in Scripture are in the life of Joshua and David.

Joshua humbly served his nation's leader, Moses. David selflessly served his nation's leader, Saul. Both of these young men (some four hundred years apart) were of no blood relation to their leaders and yet displayed biblical sonship in practical ways for us to learn from.

Moses and Saul each exhibited moments of severe lapse in their judgement; both cost the nation significantly as a result.[3] While Moses certainly maintained a greater sense of spiritual integrity than Saul, neither man was perfect.

What we see in both Joshua and David is remarkable. Both young men refused to speak poorly or act against their leader. Both young men upheld the office of their leader and preserved their sense of honour towards them.

We never once read in Scripture that Joshua passed a judgement against Moses. He always maintained a heart of service towards Moses and devotion towards God.

Even David, who was being violently pursued by Saul and eventually had to flee for his life, never spoke out against his crazed leader. In fact, he silenced Saul's critics and protected his leader's life whenever it was in his power to do so.[4]

Both of these young men were excellent spiritual "sons," and the Lord was able to move mightily through them because of it.

Learning to be a "son" is a Kingdom principle that we simply must learn, especially in this day. It is a sure path to expanding our capacity as a leader. When we recognise that those in authority over us are not perfect, we can also accept that their behaviour is not our responsibility. We will give account for our own lives. We can also then choose to adopt the position of a godly "son" who ushers in the blessing of Heaven through honour.

Among the ancient commandments passed down to the people of Israel, the very first one that had a promise of blessing attached to it was in relation to this very thing:

BLESSING FLOWS THROUGH HONOUR, AND GOD HONOURS ORDER.

> "Honour your father and mother. Then you will live a long, full life in the land the Lord your God is giving you."
>
> (Exodus 20:12 NLT)

Blessing flows through honour, and God honours order. We have the power to either facilitate or block the flow of blessing into our own lives and the lives of those around us, depending on our ability to honour those God has placed in authority over us.[5]

Spiritual sonship is a humble position that leads to blessing. In a generation where everyone wants to be "out the front" or "at the top," this is another aspect of servant

SPIRITUAL SONSHIP IS A HUMBLE POSITION THAT LEADS TO BLESSING.

leadership that reflects the heart of Jesus and manifests inner strength that is counter-cultural in our day.

Let's have a look at what it means to support those in authority over us as a means of leading those we are *responsible to*.

LIVE IN THE SECOND MILE

One of the most effective and practical methods for leading our leaders is to develop a "second mile" attitude. The "second mile" is a powerful concept Jesus taught us in the Gospels.

> "But I tell you not to resist an evil person. But whoever slaps you on your right cheek, turn the other to him also. If anyone wants to sue you and take away your tunic, let him have your cloak also. And whoever compels you to go one mile, go with him two."
>
> (Matthew 5:39–41)

In biblical times, civilians were obliged to honour the requests of their Roman superiors and military officers. If a Roman soldier were to approach a common person in the marketplace and request that he cease what he was doing to carry the officer's armour for a distance, that civilian was obliged under common law to carry out the request.

Here, Jesus is showing us the deeper heart of the Kingdom when living a life of excellence towards our authorities, whether they are spiritual or civil. He tells us to go above and beyond what is required. This is the heart of the Kingdom and the lifestyle of a follower of Jesus.

PEOPLE WHO LIVE THEIR LIVES IN THE SECOND MILE NEVER HAVE TO SEEK FAVOUR.

People who live their lives in the second mile never have to seek favour; it follows them everywhere they go. When it comes to team settings, the ones who go above and beyond are the ones leading those they are *responsible to* most effectively because they are taking ownership, initiative and bearing the load.

There is a common saying, which comically highlights the desire of a senior leader quite aptly. It says, "I'd rather cool down a zealot than warm up a corpse." There is a great sense of pleasure and relief for a senior

WE ARE CALLED TO ALWAYS BE MORE GENEROUS THAN IS REQUIRED.

leader when their teams are filled with zealous and motivated people. Perhaps in some team settings, a "check-box" or "clock-on-clock-off" mentality is satisfactory, but never in the Kingdom of God. We are called to always be more generous than is required.

Abraham is credited in both the Old and New Testaments as entertaining angels without even knowing it.[6] His default posture to extend extravagant levels of honour, generosity and hospitality on all occasions opened doors for him that he did not even know were doors until they were opened before him as positive consequences of his actions.

The account in Genesis 18 is compelling as to the nature of our responses being precursors to favour and open doors. We find Abraham exhausted, disappointed and at great levels of discomfort. The call of God had already cost him dearly, and he had spent his whole life pouring himself out for God and others. Here he is, at the age of ninety-nine, resting in the door of his tent when three men approach.

Abraham jumps to his feet and begs them to stay for a bite of bread and a drink of water. They agree, and he rushes off to prepare a banquet for them. After the three men finish dining on the elaborate feast, they suddenly reveal themselves as the Lord, and He promises both Abraham and Sarah their future son. This is the third and final confirmation of the promise Abraham first received twenty-five years prior.

Abraham had an "over-and-above" mindset. He was tired and hurting, but he jumped and ran to greet and prepare. He offered a humble serving of bread and water to these three men but proceeded to host an extravagant feast for them instead. He understated and over-performed. His default was extreme generosity.

This was Abraham's way of life. We see him willingly give the best and first choice of land to his nephew, Lot, without reservation.[7] We see him giving generously to Melchizedek a tenth of his spoils four hundred years before tithing was instituted.[8] Right through the record of Abraham's life, he is noted as being exceedingly invested, often well beyond common custom or expectation.

Jesus taught that this is indeed the way of the Kingdom.

As a method of leading those we are *responsible to*, we should take every opportunity to go above and beyond what is required and to do more than is expected. We should master what the job description stipulates, do it with excellence and then go beyond it.

It is always better to be extravagant than stingy.[9] Do not cut corners; be generous and go the second mile.

BOUNDARIES

PROFESSIONAL/PERSONAL ETIQUETTE

Dependent on a number of factors such as longevity, proximity, self-development and experience, you may find the nature of your relationship with your superiors morphing into something that resembles some aspects of friendship and familiarity.

In this case, you will need to remain aware of the boundaries required to maintain the correct order within the relationship. You will need to keep in check your understanding of how to relate to a boss who is now also a friend. This is something only you can manage, and you must do so soberly and intentionally.

Routinely pull back to reassess your etiquette in conversation, written communication and personal conduct. Be vigilant to guard against loose assumptions you may be drifting into. In your own mind, redefine the roles you each play so that you can both function in peak mode for the overall benefit of the cause.

HIGH MAINTENANCE MODE: OFF

While the onus is on our leaders to function under the revelation of servanthood and sacrifice towards us, it is not our responsibility to remind them of that, neither is it a privilege we should feel entitled to.

While he or she will be answerable to God about the way they led us, we will also be accountable to God for the way we "led" them. The writer of Hebrews instructs us very clearly that we are to pray for our leaders and make their jobs as easy as we possibly can.

> Obey your spiritual leaders, and do what they say. Their work is to watch over your souls, and they are accountable to God. Give them reason to do this with joy and not with sorrow. That would certainly not be for your benefit.
>
> (Hebrews 13:17 NLT)

When writing to Timothy, the Apostle Paul urged the Church to cover their leaders in prayer.

> I urge you, first of all, to pray for all people. Ask God to help them; intercede on their behalf, and give thanks for them. Pray this way for kings and all who are in authority so that we can live peaceful and quiet lives marked by godliness and dignity. This is good and pleases God our Saviour, who wants everyone to be saved and to understand the truth.
>
> (1 Timothy 2:1–4 NLT)

In this case, we are to be mindful of the pressures we can place on our leaders and, in turn, the pressures we should be relieving. Rather than being high maintenance team members, we should aspire to be positive, solution-oriented and supportive. Paul assures us that when we do this, the world we find ourselves located in will function more like the way it should.

The power of second is a significant leadership function, one that requires deep revelation and maturity. It is an expanded dimension of leadership that opens doors and releases opportunities to everyone involved. Let us now look at what it means to lead those we are *responsible to* through the creative ability to solve problems.

CHAPTER 12:

BE A PROBLEM SOLVER

KAROLINA GUNSSER

Leadership at any level is about solving problems. We have briefly explored this concept when leading those we are *responsible with*, but problem solving is especially crucial when building rapport and trust in the relationship between a team member and their senior leaders. There is no such gift as the gift of problem seeing. Problems are generally obvious to most people. The gift is problem solving. Great leadership seeks to find answers to problems. We need to stay creative and look for ways ahead. A senior leader's attention is immediately drawn to a team member who not only identifies problems but formulates a solution (or a number of solutions) that they are willing to action as well.

Those who lead those they are *responsible to* are problem solvers, not problem seers or problem makers, but problem solvers.

THOSE WHO LEAD THOSE THEY ARE *RESPONSIBLE TO* ARE PROBLEM SOLVERS.

A solution-oriented team member creates an advancing culture around them and therefore earns the ear and the attention of their leaders. They are not whingers and complainers, nor the ones who simply bring problems to the table; they are those who contribute answers.

Those who lead effectively in this dimension often ask themselves provoking and reflective questions like the following:

"What could be keeping my boss up at night that I might be able to resolve for them?"

"What wishes or light remarks has my leader recently made that I could action to make a reality for him?"

"What have I heard her repeatedly ask of other team members that perhaps I could step up to the plate for?"

"What makes him frustrated, and is there something I can do about it?"

"What heat could my leader be taking for the team, and how am I alleviating that pressure?"

I have made it a practice to regularly imagine what might be keeping my leaders up at night and how I might be an answer to their dilemmas. Admittedly, my leader Mark Ramsey assures me that there are very few things that rob his sleep, but you know what I am implying. I have made it a mandate to listen for subtle suggestions rather than waiting for directives. I have tried for two decades to relieve their load wherever I have the capacity to do so. I do not wait for it to be asked of me; I intentionally lean into their success and take responsibility for facilitating positive and proactive action where and when I can.

This kind of expanded leader seeks to view things through their leader's eyes.

Wasn't this what brought Joseph out from the pit and the dungeon into the palace of Egypt? It was Joseph's God-given creative ability to take ownership that brought him favour and promotion everywhere his feet landed. It should be noted that the problems he solved were always well beyond his pay grade and scope of responsibility.

Joseph solved the problems of those in authority over him time and again, earning their trust and favour. Ultimately this young man brought deliverance to a nation in crisis because of his remarkable ability to lead those he was *responsible to*. No matter the setting, Joseph went above and beyond his pay grade to serve his leaders and bring answers.

His work ethic in Potiphar's house elevated him from junior slave to house manager. Then, when false accusations landed him in the belly of an Egyptian prison, we find him again relieving pressure from the prison guards until he was called into the audience of Pharaoh himself. In due course, we see young Joseph charged with all the managerial responsibilities of the leading civilisation of the day as Prime Minister. In the face of impending national crisis, Egypt was strategically prepared and safeguarded under Joseph's leadership, whose office was second only to Pharaoh.

Though mistreated, defamed, rejected, cast aside and powerless at many times, this young man rose above his circumstances time after time, gaining favour, influence and promotion with his leaders everywhere he went. All because of his integrity, character and commitment to being an answer.

BE CREATIVE

MARK RAMSEY

There are many ways to take initiative, and one of the most dynamic ways is through the avenue of creativity. When we create, we express our heavenly DNA as children of God. The Maker of all life, Master Craftsman and Creative Genius formed us in His image to create as well. We are the most like our intended design when

TAKING INITIATIVE AND SOLVING PROBLEMS DEMANDS A CREATIVE EDGE.

we are creating. Taking initiative and solving problems demands a creative edge. When we commit to this mindset, we will often find ourselves creating something out of nothing.

Be the person who thinks outside the box. Be creative. Present new ideas, and do not become discouraged if and when your ideas are not accepted; do not let that stop you. Not all your great ideas will be accepted, and that is all right. We must continually bring new ideas to the table.

Ultimately, the ideas that are rejected or undervalued (of which there may be many) become the pathway towards the few ideas that are heard, received and materialised.

One good idea can bring change and fresh life to the organisation. One good idea may come at the expense of one hundred lesser ideas, but the whole process will have been worth it for change and ingenuity. Be the person committed to bringing those ideas.

Every time we come to putting together a new Citipointe Worship album, we collect thirty or forty songs from our locations around the world. Every contributor and songwriter knows that only a dozen songs will make it onto the album. Incredibly, this process never hinders the creativity and zeal of our songwriters in producing another collection of powerful songs year after year.

A person who expands their leadership capacity to influence those they are *responsible to* will keep bringing ideas to the table, even if some of them are not picked up. Leaders create. Leaders dream. Leaders are problem solvers who take initiative.

A senior leader must make it a goal and a joy to create room for the people in their organisation to keep bringing ideas to the table. This kind of senior leader is governed by an instinct that at any given moment, someone on the team may submit a new idea that could potentially be a game-changer for the organisation.

It is worth noting at this point that "glory-grabbing" will stifle our ability to lead in any direction, but especially in this dimension of leadership. The right we sometimes feel entitled to hold over the intellectual property of our creative ideas may rob us (and the organisation) of a genuine and full creative experience.

Submitting a good idea to your senior leader may have appeared fruitless at the time, but you may find months later, after a lengthy incubation period, that he or she announces a bright new initiative sounding remarkably like the pitch you made some time back. The idea may very well have been yours, but if your motive is right, you will concern yourself less with the glory of the idea and more with the impact that idea will have on the furthering of the mission. Similarly, when the senior leader is leading their team well, they will acknowledge the source of the idea, and team trust is built in a powerful way and reinforced from both directions.

What we do in those moments is realise that we have, in essence, led the leader and brought change beyond our pay grade. Leadership is not about prominence; it is about influence. It might have been your idea, but it really does not matter who gets the credit. Continue to seed great ideas with your leaders, and you will see incredible benefits come in the future.

LEADERSHIP IS NOT ABOUT PROMINENCE; IT IS ABOUT INFLUENCE.

Be creative. Think outside the box. Never stop dreaming, imagining and challenging the status quo. You will lead those you are *responsible to* when you become that person.

WHAT PROBLEM SOLVERS BELIEVE

KAROLINA GUNSSER

Problem solvers can be a rare breed to come by. The functions of thinking creatively and challenging the norm employ mindsets and behaviours that can be invigorating for some and unsettling for others. Problem solvers are set apart by their core belief systems. These types of leaders are informed by three distinct values that we will now explore.

I TAKE OWNERSHIP

Firstly, problem solvers have a foundational value for ownership. This motivates an individual to take personal responsibility for the world around them. Ownership moves them beyond bare-minimum-thinking because their vested interests run deep.

The scriptural context here is cited in Jesus' narrative, which contrasts shepherds and hirelings. The passage in the tenth chapter of John's gospel is rich with many spiritual connotations of the Father's devotion to us, His sheep. However, for the sake of staying on topic here, we will focus on the ownership and personal responsibility illustrated in verses 11 through 13.

> "I am the good shepherd. The good shepherd gives His life for the sheep. But a hireling, he who is not the shepherd, one who does not own the sheep, sees the wolf coming and leaves the sheep and flees; and the wolf catches the sheep and scatters them. The hireling flees because he is a hireling and does not care about the sheep."

(John 10:11–13)

Jesus continues in the following verses to explain His sonship to the Father by His self-sacrificial devotion to the Father's sheep, which of course are us. Jesus is modelling for us the stark difference between a son and a hireling. Someone who is a son or daughter of the vision will give willingly and without restraint because they carry a deep sense of personal ownership. A hireling clocks on and clocks off without ever going beyond the bare minimum of what is required in their job description. A son understands he has an inheritance, an eternal

SOMEONE WHO IS A SON OR DAUGHTER OF THE VISION WILL GIVE WILLINGLY AND WITHOUT RESTRAINT BECAUSE THEY CARRY A DEEP SENSE OF PERSONAL OWNERSHIP.

reward; a hireling only seeks a week-to-week compensation for minimum effort.

Scripture is filled with the truths of sonship; it is, in fact, a vital and foundational Kingdom principle, as we have explored in the previous chapter. Our understanding can also go beyond the concept of *hirelings* to draw a contrast between sons and *slaves*.

From the outside, the activities conducted by a son, a hireling or a slave may all appear to be similar. It can be difficult to distinguish which of the three characters we are encountering by only observing their deeds or accomplishments. Frequently, slaves and sons work equally as hard. The true test, then, is one that only the Father can measure in honesty within the heart of the person.

As mentioned previously, sonship is a revelation. Sonship is a conviction. A slave is weighed down by ill-fitting burdens. A hireling accepts no burden of responsibility. Both extremes are opposed to heavenly ownership.

While a son supersedes them both, sonship simultaneously applies spiritual discipline (not the striving of a slave) and walks in freedom (not the complacency of a hireling). A son carries his position with strength and grace. A wise son is a blessing to his father.[1] A wise son leads his superiors by taking initiative and taking responsibility.

The motive of a person is tested in the face of danger or threat, as cited in this parable. A son takes personal responsibility, while the others abandon post and leave the problem to someone else.

When something needs to be done, this type of expanded leader does not wait for anyone else; they step up themselves. This requires a deeper sense of stewardship of the corporate call and vision. It can be as simple as believing that a piece of litter is not only the janitor's responsibility but mine as well. It is a deep sense of initiative. People who take ownership will attract the eye and ear of their leader. When they take responsibility and ownership like this, the leader's ear turns their way because their genuine actions have built trust and earned the right to be heard.

For example, a person's function might be outworked in the marketing department, but if there is litter in the Church car park, this team member should not step over the rubbish, leaving it for someone else to deal with at another time. It may not be in their job description to collect and manage on-site waste, but because they carry a level of organisational ownership that transcends checklists, they immediately collect the litter and dispose of it appropriately.

In organisational structures, this plays out in the relationships between leaders and their followers, based on the foundation of mutual service of one another. This is the fundamental concept of this whole book. Leading in any dimension requires self-sacrifice and service to the other person.

I TAKE INITIATIVE

Secondly, problem solvers intrinsically believe that opportunity is tucked away within every problem.[2] Therefore, the solution is already present somewhere, just waiting to be uncovered and executed. Moreover, they believe that the opportunities are up for grabs to anyone who will take them, so they instinctively step up to the plate and act. These people are rarely plagued by analysis paralysis since their core belief reminds them that the opportunity of a lifetime only lasts the lifetime of the opportunity.[3]

THE OPPORTUNITY OF A LIFETIME ONLY LASTS THE LIFETIME OF THE OPPORTUNITY.

An obvious means of problem solving is initiative. Without taking initiative, we run the risk of overstating and under-performing and becoming all talk with no action. When a follower takes initiative and displays genuine ownership, the weight carried by the senior leader is leveraged and lightened. This creates space for the senior leader to stretch further on behalf of the organisation because their hands are being freed up. Seeing an opportunity and taking initiative allows a follower to lead their leader into the future.

What you walk past, you approve of. Turning a blind eye to or leaving a known problem to someone else are the behavioural habits of those who are most likely not going to earn the privilege of influencing their leaders.

WHAT YOU WALK PAST, YOU APPROVE OF.

When something needs to be done, we get it done. We must decide that there will never come a time in the future when we are too big for the small things.[4] Regardless of our job description, we are contributors to the greater whole of the organisation, and so we take ownership of the vision at large.

> Therefore, to him who knows to do good and does not do it, to him it is sin.

> (James 4:17)

James taught us that we cannot do everything, but we can do something, and that thing we must do. Failing to do it is sin. Proverbs even teaches in several instances not to put off until tomorrow what can be done today.[5] Taking initiative assumes both a highly responsive stance and a sense of urgency.

I SERVE OTHERS

Thirdly, at their very core, problem solvers believe that the greatest call of leadership is to serve. They vigilantly and decisively expel all narcissistic notions that would draw their efforts to self, and they look to satisfy the needs of others. Being others-oriented is the only true pathway to solution-based thinking.

Problem solving is a commitment to serve others. It moves a person's focus away from introspection—where they are the centre and focus of their awareness—towards the needs and

PROBLEM SOLVING IS A COMMITMENT TO SERVE OTHERS.

efforts of others. A problem solver is attentive to what is going on in the world around them and the part they can play within it for the overall betterment of all involved. A problem solver's broad perspective allows them to "see" and serve others. We have already cited Jesus' words to His disciples about becoming the least in order to find greatness.

> "...the greatest honour and authority is reserved for the one with the heart of a servant. For even the Son of Man did not come expecting to be served by everyone, but to serve everyone, and to give his life in exchange for the salvation of many."

> (Matthew 20:27–28 TPT)

Here is our model and blueprint for leadership. This is the kind of posture that allows a person to readily influence the world around them. A person who truly serves others builds confidence in every dimension of leadership. In a team setting, they are the ones who lead those they are *responsible to* and become known by their leaders as trustworthy and vision-filled team members.

But how do we interact with our superiors in a culture that questions authority figures? What does God say about those in positions of authority over us? Let's answer those questions in the next chapter.

CHAPTER 13:

GIVE HONOUR

KAROLINA GUNSSER

In many western cultures, we have fallen into the trap of contempt and familiarity towards those in positions of leadership over us. Perhaps one of the downfalls of democracy is the disrespect that is tolerated, even celebrated, towards anyone of a differing opinion, even if that person is an authority figure. This is dangerous ground.

We see this vividly in Mark and Matthew's accounts of Jesus' restricted ministry in His hometown. Coming into Nazareth, fresh off the back of such great miracles as raising a dead girl to life, delivering a demon-possessed man and healing a woman with a twelve-year blood condition, Jesus' power was immediately neutralised by the contempt and scorn of those who knew Him best. His school friends, childhood neighbours and family friends were offended that He was displaying power and authority. They could not fathom the possibility that someone they knew so well would surpass them in any way. Their familiarity with Jesus bred contempt, and that contempt limited the miraculous.

> But Jesus said to them, "A prophet is not without honour except in his own country, among his own relatives, and in his own house." Now He could do no mighty work there, except that He laid His hands on a few sick people and healed them. And He marvelled because of their unbelief. Then He went about the villages in a circuit, teaching.
>
> (Mark 6:4–6)

FAMILIARITY IN ANY MEASURE STUNTS WHAT GOD CAN DO.

It should be both astounding and sobering to us all that the Son of God would be limited in any way, and that limitation came from the attitudes of those around Him. Familiarity in any measure stunts what God can do.

This account is a stark contrast to what we see in the eighth chapter of Matthew's gospel regarding the faith of the Roman Centurion. Here we find a man who was not akin to Jesus, not a Jew, not culturally related, having more honour than his own countrymen.

Perhaps the Centurion recognised one thing he shared in common with this man of miracles, and that was authority. The Centurion soldier came to Jesus with a request that was tethered to a great deal of respect.

> Now when Jesus had entered Capernaum, a centurion came to Him, pleading with Him, saying, "Lord, my servant is lying at home paralysed, dreadfully tormented."
>
> And Jesus said to him, "I will come and heal him."
>
> The centurion answered and said, "Lord, I am not worthy that You should come under my roof. But only speak a word, and my servant will be healed. For I also am a man under authority, having soldiers under me. And I say to

this one, 'Go,' and he goes; and to another, 'Come,' and he comes; and to my servant, 'Do this,' and he does it."

When Jesus heard it, He marvelled, and said to those who followed,

"Assuredly, I say to you, I have not found such great faith, not even in Israel! And I say to you that many will come from east and west, and sit down with Abraham, Isaac, and Jacob in the kingdom of heaven. But the sons of the kingdom will be cast out into outer darkness. There will be weeping and gnashing of teeth." Then Jesus said to the centurion, "Go your way; and as you have believed, so let it be done for you." And his servant was healed that same hour.

(Matthew 8:5–13)

In Jesus' time, much of the known world was under Roman rule, a highly organised and systematic regime. Law enforcement was carried out by the armed forces and broken down into ranks and groups. A Roman legion consisted of 6,000 soldiers. Within that legion were appointed proven soldiers called Centurions who were in charge of one hundred men each (a century). Each legion contained sixty Roman Centurions who were deeply revered and respected as leaders of absolute authority.

In this record, we find a soldier resolutely convinced about the power of authority to bring effectual activity and change. He was so convinced, in fact, that when he heard rumours of miraculous potential, he superimposed his pragmatic core beliefs about natural authority over the supernatural possibilities and approached Jesus with full confidence that just one word could rearrange his dire realities.

Jesus marvelled.
And Jesus moved.
Miraculously.

God flows through channels of honour, and God honours order. Honour cannot be demanded. Honour is earned, and it is

OBEDIENCE CAN BE DEMANDED, BUT HONOUR CANNOT. voluntarily ascribed to one worthy of it. Obedience can be demanded, but honour cannot.

As we host leaders above us, we hold executive power to determine what we receive from them. A faulty heart attitude will block us from the miraculous and diminish the covering offered to us by God through our leaders. When we cultivate a culture of honour, we position our hearts to receive.

One of the ways we do this in our worship services around the world is by standing and applauding the Word of God as the preacher makes their way to the platform. We understand that the

WHEN WE CULTIVATE A CULTURE OF HONOUR, WE POSITION OUR HEARTS TO RECEIVE. person is not seeking notoriety or applause, but because they carry the Word of God to us for that time, what they carry has the power to transform us if our hearts are postured to receive. In the many thousands of Church services held every year around the world, Citipointe Church members stand every time to honour the Word before it is delivered by our preachers. We have a belief that what you honour, you can receive from.

We also hold our guests in high esteem for this same reason because it sets an atmosphere of faith for the miraculous and for salvation. When we honour our leaders and guests, our attitudes, actions, and words convey a powerful message: "I am expectant of what God can bring to my life through you." This message gives the person confidence and room to give more of themselves; it draws the best out of them.

We have the power to determine the degree of spiritual impartation that our leaders and guests will deliver to our lives, teams, churches and communities.

SPACE FOR THE MIRACULOUS

It has been said a few times in this book already that when one person on the team wins, it is a win for all. In the case of leading those we are *responsible to*, when we contribute to our leader's success, we propel them further ahead, and this immediately creates a void within the organisation that pulls everyone else forward.

Conversely, when our leader is held down with issues that other team members are capable of and should be handling themselves, the progress of the organisation is significantly slowed down. In this case, no one is winning.

When the senior leader's hands are filled with non-essential tasks, it means that they cannot pick up the more weighty things, which are required to advance and take ground on behalf of those they are leading—us!

There are some things only the leader has authority to do on behalf of the people they are leading. Of course, there are many things that the leader has the ability to do, but by releasing your leaders of such things, they are then able to use their finite capacity on things only they can do. When we release our leaders, we create room. In the Kingdom, that room is often miraculous.

WHEN WE RELEASE OUR LEADERS, WE CREATE ROOM. IN THE KINGDOM, THAT ROOM IS OFTEN MIRACULOUS.

Perhaps this mindset is more spiritual than practical in nature because it is a matter of understanding spiritual authority and anointing. It is an understanding of the way God flows through His appointed channels. These revelations compel a follower to release their senior leader to lead in the way only he or she can.

SPEAK WELL OF YOUR LEADER

A powerful way to lead those you are *responsible to* is to ensure we speak well of our leaders at all times. Words can be subtler than actions but equally as powerful. Our words create worlds. We have all seen first-hand the power of language to build and strengthen culture or tear it down.

OUR WORDS CREATE WORLDS.

Proverbs tells us that life and death are in the power of the tongue.[1] In effect, we can assassinate people with our words. What is even more sobering is that every time we speak words of death about another person, we agree with the accuser rather than our Saviour. It is the enemy who comes to steal, kill and destroy, while Jesus brings abundant life.[2] We must be increasingly aware of who our words agree with—the accuser or the Spirit of God.

> "A good man out of the good treasure of his heart brings forth good; and an evil man out of the evil treasure of his heart brings forth evil. For out of the abundance of the heart his mouth speaks."
>
> (Luke 6:45)

The way we speak tells a whole lot about the condition of our hearts. A major part of leadership is cultivating good heart health, which we will explore in the final section of this book. However, the way we speak about our leaders also evidences our true belief about God.

> If someone says, "I love God," and hates his brother, he is a liar; for he who does not love his brother whom he has seen, how can he love God whom he has not seen?
>
> (1 John 4:20)

God is our ultimate authority and the One we follow above all others. We practice our submission and love towards Him here in our earthly relationships. As parents, we try to instil respect for authority in our children because we know this will serve them as adults in their capacity to obey and submit to God.

Jesus reminded us that we are proven trustworthy by the way we manage what belongs to another person and what we do with the seemingly small and insignificant beginnings.

> "He who is faithful in what is least is faithful also in much; and he who is unjust in what is least is unjust also in much...."
>
> "And if you have not been faithful in what is another man's, who will give you what is your own?"

(Luke 16:10, 12)

In all his heartache with King Saul, David never spoke out against him. And when those around him spoke out of turn about the king, David was quick to correct the conversation. Sabotage and complaining is never the way of leadership, not in the Kingdom anyway. God was able to elevate David because he had proven himself trustworthy through many years honouring his leader.

There may be instances when you find yourself at odds with your leaders. If you have an issue with them, you should see them personally and respectfully. It is entirely possible to voice a disagreement or present a challenge in a respectful and honouring manner.

Once we have voiced our position, we then step back from the situation, knowing that we have done our part as honourably as possible. God will hold our leaders accountable for the responsibilities in their sphere of influence, and He will hold us accountable for ours.

We must make sure to never go against them publicly or in private conversations. Wherever we go, we must commit to ensuring our leader is being lifted up.

LEARN YOUR LEADER

In reality, we can never fully grasp the weight our leaders carry. Understanding the mind of your leader will cause you to grow and develop a sense of empathy for the heat they take for you and the team regularly.

We can be prone to passing judgements far too easily. We form opinions on how and why things might be done, with the limited understanding we hold to filter what we see and experience. Only as our own leadership responsibility deepens do we begin to more appropriately appreciate the decisions our leaders before us have made.

Leading those we are *responsible to* is a resolve to loyalty. It is a commitment to bear weight, arms and responsibility for our leader. To do this well, we do our best to understand the leaders above us. We learn how they operate and how they think so that we can come into the slipstream of the current they are creating.

There are countless personality profiles and assessments we can study to learn the different ways people are "wired." As well as learning about ourselves, we can more aptly understand others and how to work with them in ways that maximise their strengths and defaults. When we harness these practical tools available at our fingertips, together with a genuine commitment to longevity and loyalty, we can come to discern our leader. This is crucial to expanding ourselves in this dimension of leadership.

Hearing and actioning the subtle remarks of our leader is a spiritual privilege. David, a clear leadership role model, was an unassuming and humble captain. His men were trophies of transformation under his leadership. Once self-seeking criminals, David's mighty men became a unified force to be reckoned with.

One difficult night, David and his men found themselves hiding just a short distance from enemy lines. As they settled for the night, the men heard David wishfully crave for a drink of water from the well of Bethlehem. As David drifted off to sleep, his men broke through enemy lines to draw a cup of water from the well and brought it back to their leader. Not a command, not a directive, not explicitly stated in a job description; it was just a whisper, a comment amongst friends.

The level of sacrifice they were willing to express on his behalf astounded David. So moved, so humbled, so unsettled by their gesture, David poured the water out before the Lord as a drink offering.

> "The Lord forbid that I should drink this!" he exclaimed. "This water is as precious as the blood of these men who risked their lives to bring it to me." So David did not drink it.
>
> (2 Samuel 23:17 NLT)

What did the selfless act of these men do in the heart of their leader? It broke David's heart all the more for his men and for his responsibility under God to lead them well. True servanthood brings the very best out of people.

Here, David's men selflessly discerned the heart's desire of their leader, and he responded by becoming even more humbled and committed to his mandate.

TRUE SERVANTHOOD BRINGS THE VERY BEST OUT OF PEOPLE.

A foolish junior leader wants only to be understood and validated, while a wise junior leader will seek to understand and learn.

A foolish junior leader wants to be seen, while a wise junior leader watches, interprets and acts in accordance.

A foolish junior leader waits for expressed directions, while a wise junior leader listens carefully for subtle suggestions, wishes and off-the-cuff remarks made by their senior leader that they can put into action without being asked.

You should be able to "read" your leader—their body language, their non-verbal cues and the under-tone of the verbal ones too.

Before we moved to lead our own location, Sam and I were assistant pastors within the home location in Brisbane, Australia, serving directly with Pastors Mark and Leigh Ramsey. Over the years, we sought to serve them in greater ways. We would position ourselves in Sunday worship services where we could watch Pastor Mark. We learned his body language. We knew by the way he shifted in his seat what his posture meant. When he noticed something in the service that made him uneasy, we would make it our business to inconspicuously action a solution immediately. We decided that while his job was to carry the spiritual weight of the service, we would lighten the load wherever we could. In doing so, we released him to carry his weight with ease, and we allowed the spiritual dynamic of the service to flow unhindered.

There have been many other initiatives I have started after hearing Pastor Mark's "wouldn't it be nice if..." remarks. Although many of these initiatives fell outside my immediate portfolio of responsibilities, I saw them as opportunities to help bring my leader's vision to fruition and to expand my own capacity through serving him in that manner. When he wins, I win.

We have now explored three of the four dimensions of leadership available to us. At this point, the myth of single-dimensional leadership has been challenged in our thinking, and we are conceptualising a more expanded approach to our personal leadership practice. At this stage, we are now ready to investigate the most pivotal aspect of our personal leadership methods—the leading of self: the only person you will ever be *responsible for*.

LEADING THOSE I AM RESPONSIBLE TO

PERSONAL REFLECTION:

Senior leader, what are your strengths,
and what are your weaknesses?

Junior leader, what's the best way to submit, even if you
think your idea is better than those being proposed?

Subtle Requests

Why is it important to detect and respond to the
subtle requests of my leader?

Thinking Like My Leader
How can I learn to think like my leader
when I am making decisions?

Releasing My Leader
How can I always speak life about my leader,
even when they aren't in the room?

Relational Leader
Why is it vital to see my leader as friendly
but not confuse it for friendship?

PART FOUR:

LEADING THE PERSON I AM
RESPONSIBLE FOR

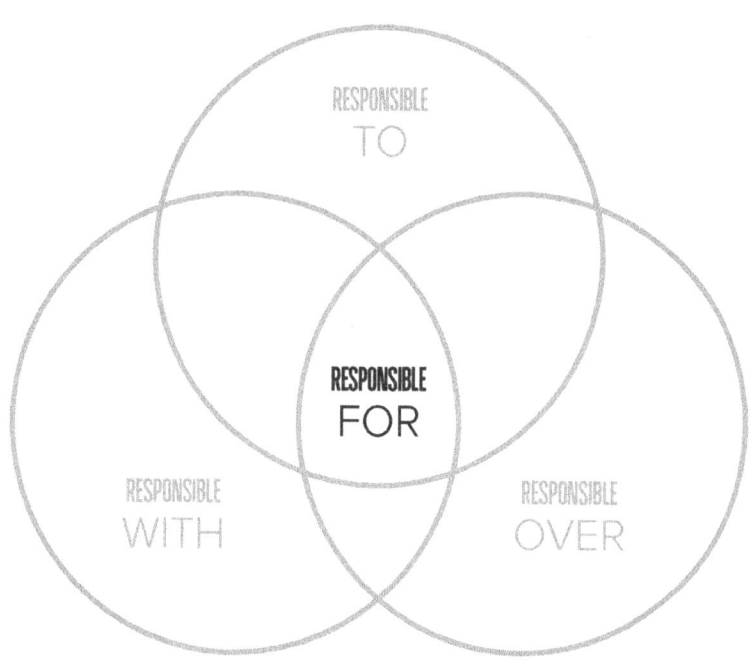

(PROVERBS 25:28)

Whoever has no rule over his own spirit
Is like a city broken down, without walls.

"When wealth is lost, nothing is lost.
When health is lost, something is lost.
When character is lost, all is lost."

– BILLY GRAHAM

CHAPTER 14:

THE PERSON IN THE MIRROR

KAROLINA GUNSSER

So far, we have looked at three of four dimensions of leadership. We have broken the great leadership myth that leading those you are *responsible over* is the only way to lead. In this section, we will explore the fourth and most significant dimension of leadership—leading ourselves. Truly, the other three dimensions are rendered obsolete in the absence of appropriate self-leadership. If we want to be expanded leaders who can lead in the other three dimensions, it is paramount that we learn self-leadership.

You are the only person you will ever be responsible for. The other three dimensions of leadership are external to self. However, self-leadership understands that there are

YOU ARE THE ONLY PERSON YOU WILL EVER BE RESPONSIBLE FOR.

no "others" involved here. You are not responsible "for" anyone else but yourself, and if we do not lead ourselves, the other three dimensions fall apart. A lack of self-leadership will result in the other three dimensions being completely ineffective over time. There are no shortcuts. We must effectively lead ourselves.

FAITHFULNESS OF HEART

KAROLINA GUNSSER

As Christian leaders, we long to please our Heavenly Father in such a way that He will one day greet us with the words, "Well done, good and faithful servant."[1] If we are not careful, when we consider the words "faithful" and "faithfulness," we can promptly recall our deeds, functions or exploits as evidence of our faithfulness. It is a part of our human nature to lean into works and striving as an immediate measure of worth and validation.

However, the condition of our hearts matters more to God than our exploits for Him. When God measured the success of the great kings of old in Israelite history, He used only one criteria of assessment. Over and over in the Old Testament, we find God defining the kings of Israel and Judah according to their "faithfulness of heart."[2]

THE CONDITION OF OUR HEARTS MATTERS MORE TO GOD THAN OUR EXPLOITS FOR HIM.

This word "faithful" is most appropriately understood in a marriage context, where God measures the effect of our lives according to our faithfulness towards Him through exclusive devotion, like that of a wife towards her husband and vice versa. He measured the kings as either faithful or adulterous in their hearts. Many kings of Israel and Judah were lured away by false gods, pride, riches and fame. A few kings determined to set their hearts on the ways of God and honouring His name above all other temptations and trends in their generation. God called them faithful.

Leading ourselves is a leadership of the heart, and that towards God alone. Could that heavenly greeting, "Well done, good and faithful servant," be understood more accurately through the lens of marriage and intimacy rather than metrics and results alone? God would desire to welcome us back as undefiled lovers who lived lives of exclusive devotion to Him.

He desires to welcome us home, saying, "Well done! You remained faithful to our relationship. You resisted temptations from all fronts, and you remained true to our covenant of love for each other. Well done! Your life is a powerful testament to what happens when God and man remain faithfully devoted to each other."

Overall, the "faithful" kings were significantly more effective in their leadership functions than those God measured as "unfaithful." They attracted the favour of God Himself, who stepped in on their behalf on many occasions to bring about supernatural outcomes for the nation. Effective leadership in the Kingdom of God begins in the hearts of men and women who are faithful; they become gracious recipients of His favour and His pleasure.

> **EFFECTIVE LEADERSHIP IN THE KINGDOM OF GOD BEGINS IN THE HEARTS OF MEN AND WOMEN WHO ARE FAITHFUL.**

DISCOVERING GOD'S WILL

MARK RAMSEY

As we commit our hearts to the path towards greater dimensions in God and continue to give our lives for the cause of Christ to see people saved, healed and set free, then we must commit to the process of being expanded into bigger and stronger leaders in the Kingdom of God. We cannot afford to just look at one aspect of our leadership. We need to believe we can be bigger than we are right now.

> **WE NEED TO BELIEVE WE CAN BE BIGGER THAN WE ARE RIGHT NOW.**

This fourth section on leading the person you are *responsible for* is undergirded by a passage in Paul's letter to the Church in Rome. It covers three aspects specifically pertaining to self-leadership. If you have ever wondered about the will of God for your life, then this is the verse you have been searching for.

> I beseech you therefore, brethren, by the mercies of God, that you present your bodies a living sacrifice, holy, acceptable to God, which is your reasonable service. And do not be conformed to this world, but be transformed by the renewing of your mind, that you may prove what is that good and acceptable and perfect will of God.

(Romans 12:1–2)

If you allow yourself to follow the path in that verse, you will never have to worry about whether or not you are in the will of God. Becoming the person these two verses describe ensures that you will lead yourself effectively and remain right in the middle of where God wants you to be.

To present our lives as living sacrifices to God means doing so in every moment of every day. From working to recreation, we are to remain surrendered to the purposes of God. This passage further encourages us to allow the spirit of our mind to be renewed daily according to God's Word. When we do these two things, we lead ourselves into the will of God. It really is as simple as that.

Many people are concerned about what God has for them in the future. We do not need to know the full blueprint of what lies in wait for us in the future. Remaining in the perfect will of God requires that we are transformed by the renewing of our mind and that we present our whole life as a living sacrifice on a daily basis.

Once we have positioned ourselves that way, God can lead us to our destiny. He can lead us to fulfil our potential, achieve the impossible and meet every outcome He has intended for us.

When we unpack Romans 12:1–2 a little further, we can see that self-leadership means taking *responsibility for* ourselves in the following three ways:

PRESENT YOURSELF

You are a triune being, an image bearer and a multifaceted creation. You exist as body, soul and spirit. Before we explore all three dimensions, we must recognise that to present our life back to God is a conscious act of surrender—a deliberate choice. We must consciously move in a particular direction, in this case, God's direction. Otherwise, our subconscious self will lead us to undesired places.

Our lives are not our own. God created us and made us stewards of our lives; all we are and all we have. In return, we are called to "present" who we are and what

OUR LIVES ARE NOT OUR OWN.

we have back to Him—for He is the One we originated from and the One who knows the way everything functions best. To resist such surrender is both foolish and an act of self-sabotage.

DO NOT BE CONFORMED

When we know who we are and *whose* we are, the pressures and cultures around us do not sway us. We can hold our own convictions and identity in the midst of any circumstance or environment. This resolve addresses our motivations: the "why" behind the "what"—why we do what we do. This

WHEN WE KNOW WHO WE ARE AND *WHOSE* WE ARE, THE PRESSURES AND CULTURES AROUND US DO NOT SWAY US.

is our driving force, our true north. Without defining or perhaps diagnosing our motives, we are subject to all kinds of influences. However, when we have effectively conformed our motivations to the will of God and our minds have been renewed to desire His intentions in and through us, then self-leadership takes on powerful possibilities.

BE TRANSFORMED

Each one of us is on a journey—sanctification does not happen overnight. In one moment, the Spirit of God brings us eternal salvation and then takes a lifetime to transform us from glory to glory. Scripture tells us that we are to "work out our salvation"[3] as we are transformed "from glory to glory."[4] That is good news for all of us.

On this side of eternity, we never truly "arrive." Yes, salvation is received at the moment of repentance and is all encompassing, but we all know that "Monday is coming," bringing with it the demands of spiritual regeneration for the life of good works we are called to live.[5] Transformation is done by and in the Spirit of God, starting in the spirit of the mind and outworking through our choices and behaviours.

These truths require a great sense of self-awareness and self-control. The foundation of all great leadership is the ability to lead one's self.

Let's look more closely at these three ideas.

CHAPTER 15:

PRESENT YOURSELF

MARK RAMSEY

Coined as the wisest man in history, King Solomon wrote a book of the Bible almost entirely dedicated to this theme of self-leadership. Much of the book of Proverbs lends its principles to the idea of wisdom and the way wisdom guides our thoughts, attitudes and actions.

When Solomon described our state of being, he likened us to cities.

> Whoever has no rule over his own spirit
> Is like a city broken down, without walls.

(Proverbs 25:28)

Large walls commonly surrounded the cities that existed during the days when the book of Proverbs was written. Back then, a city with no walls to protect it was easily susceptible to invasion and attack. There was no rest, peace or confidence in cities like that. The people calling those types of cities home most likely lived in fear and anxiety.

Solomon drew a compelling similarity between cities and our souls; both required fortification for survival, prosperity and peace. He concluded that while the walls of a city were built with bricks and mortar, the fortification of the soul was built by self-control. The soul without self-control is like a city broken down without walls, frequently invaded by the enemy.

At this point, it is important to define what the soul is. Just as we are triune beings made up of a body, a soul and a spirit, our soul itself also has three dimensions. Our souls are made up of our mind, our will and our emotions. Immediately, we can acknowledge from personal experience and from the observation of others that without deliberate leadership over our mind, will and emotions, we are in big trouble.

Understanding the intricacies of our own lives allows for greater self-awareness and, in turn, more effective self-leadership. People who have self-control build up the walls of the soul by the wisdom of the Spirit; this is the beginning of their self-leadership. The better their ability to lead self, the better their ability to express leadership through the other dimensions and spheres of their lives.

The picture is this: a city with broken-down walls is vulnerable to everything and anything that comes its way. Invading groups can pillage, kill and destroy. The inhabitants have no defensive options available to them. Scripture is telling us that a person who has no control over his or her own self is like that city. Enemy forces can come in and steal from that person at any time. The enemy avails himself to the plunder—things like identity, joy, purpose, the plans and promises of God, and anything else of value and eternal significance.

BE ALWAYS BUILDING

MARK RAMSEY

We have to intentionally and diligently build spiritual walls around our own lives so that we can lead ourselves. Spiritual fortification allows us to make sure we are not standing vulnerably in the face of our circumstances and experiences. A person who does not or will not take control over self will be led every which way. Self-leadership is a continual decision-making process to cultivate the spiritual fruit of self-control and not be out of control.

A PERSON WHO DOES NOT OR WILL NOT TAKE CONTROL OVER SELF WILL BE LED EVERY WHICH WAY.

When we don't take control, we often make excuses such as, "It's just my personality," or "I just can't help myself." The truth is, you really can help yourself; you just do not truly want to. If every time you got angry, someone inflicted some sort of physical pain, you would only be angry once, maybe twice, maybe three times if you were a slow learner. But almost certainly, you would change your response to avoid the pain being inflicted on you.

The right stimulus is all we need to change. When we finally realise that the pain of staying the same outweighs the pain of change, we are willing to begin the process.

WHEN WE FINALLY REALISE THAT THE PAIN OF STAYING THE SAME OUTWEIGHS THE PAIN OF CHANGE, WE ARE WILLING TO BEGIN THE PROCESS.

It has been said that the definition of a lunatic is someone who does the same things over and over, hoping for a different result. We wonder why things are not changing, why we are not growing, why we are hitting ceilings in our lives and not stepping fully into what we know God has for us. Yet, we continue to do and think the same things we always have.

MOVING FORWARD IN LIFE REQUIRES FREQUENT EVALUATION AND RESHUFFLING.

Moving forward in life requires frequent evaluation and reshuffling. If you do what you have always done, you will keep getting the results you have always had. Your existing mindsets and behaviours have served you to this point but may need adjusting in order to move you into greater depths of your potential. Self-control affords you the ability to fortify your soul and secure the future God has for you. Self-control allows you to move beyond mindsets and behaviours that have limited you in the past.

THE STIMULUS FOR CHANGE IS REALISING WHO YOU ARE AS A SON OR DAUGHTER OF GOD.

In the Kingdom, the stimulus for change is realising who you are as a son or daughter of God. Read that sentence again.

This revelation allows you to reject false identities and directs you into your proper position in Christ. When we make this leap into godly identity, we are now talking about a solid foundation and the type of fortification that builds the Kingdom of Heaven into our lives.

If we want to gain self-control, then we must live out of who we are called to be, not the circumstances we were born into or even how we were raised. Even the best of earthly parents are still human beings with shortcomings; it is not so with our Heavenly Father who calls us His own. God has called us to be His children. Once we live in that place, we can start to take control of ourselves, not by trying harder but by realising our identity as sons and daughters of God. If we do not get that right, we will forever be striving and struggling in our ability to exercise self-control.

To illustrate this concept, and before we get into the practical aspects of leading the person you are *responsible for*, let us look at just a few common areas people struggle to lead themselves and why.

Punctuality is a leadership issue. If you are usually late, your life is out of control. Of course, there are sometimes exceptional circumstances that impact our schedules, but if you are continually late, then you have a self-leadership issue to address. You are not in control of who you are.

Pornography is a leadership issue. You see, sex is not evil until it is out of order, out of control and out of the will of God. God originally intended sex for blessing, intimacy and fruitfulness. However, a lack of control allows the perversion and corruption of even the God-ordained things in this life (such as sexual intimacy), leaving us bound and enslaved by destructive habits and cravings.

Gluttony is a leadership issue. Nothing should be able to make you eat more than you should. Food is a leadership issue. Take control and say "no" when you need to. You will lead better in the other three dimensions of leadership when you live a life of inner strength. Walking the talk always comes down to self-leadership and makes you a more credible leader. To become the change we want to see in the world, we must first lead ourselves and know who we are as God's sons and daughters.

How do we lead ourselves in a practical and personal sense? It is easy enough to grasp the concept; however, if the application were just as easy, more people would be doing it. In the following sections, we will explore some useful ways to lead ourselves with success and tangible results.

BE AUTHENTIC
KAROLINA GUNSSER

You have three faces. You have a public face that everyone sees. You have a private face that only your spouse, children, close family and selected friends will see. You also have a third face, and that is your secret face, the face that no one else sees but God. Leading self is about those last two aspects—the private and the secret. You need to know that they are the most important areas to cultivate. Ultimately, if you have not cultivated your private and secret worlds, evidence of that neglect will certainly show in due course. It is only a matter of time before the cracks of your inner world will eventually start to present themselves in the outer dimensions of your life.[1]

Jesus talked to the crowd about this in the sixth chapter of Matthew's gospel. He warned us not to show off and do things on the street corners like the hypocrites do, but to make sure that we are doing the majority of our significant activity in the private realms of our lives.

Jesus urged us to ensure that what we are doing for God is done in private and not for the acclamation of man. He talked about doing good to please God. We should not let our right hand know what our left hand is doing. He warned us against praying with vain and repetitious words for show and to gain acclamation from a human audience. He called us to the standard where our private world is authentic, humble and motivated by the correct desires.

When we seek the acclamation of man and receive it, that is the end of the equation; we already have our reward. But when we do something in private, it is just the beginning. God who sees in private will work supernaturally on our efforts to bring change to the world and finally reward us eternally. We can all admit that it is much greater to receive a reward from God than man.

IT IS MUCH GREATER TO RECEIVE A REWARD FROM GOD THAN MAN.

BE WATCHFUL

KAROLINA GUNSSER

The private and secret faces are cultivated in the heart. In the Bible, the word "heart" is often interchangeable with the terms "soul" or "mind." Scripture after Scripture teaches, warns, urges and encourages us to pay close attention to the health of our hearts for the well-being of our lives.

Keep your heart with all diligence,

For out of it spring the issues of life.

(Proverbs 4:23)

Every way of a man is right in his own eyes,

But the Lord weighs the hearts.

(Proverbs 21:2)

"A good man out of the good treasure of his heart brings forth good; and an evil man out of the evil treasure of his heart brings forth evil. For out of the abundance of the heart his mouth speaks."

(Luke 6:45)

"Blessed are the pure in heart,

For they shall see God."

(Matthew 5:8)

Let the words of my mouth and the meditation of my heart

Be acceptable in Your sight,

O Lord, my strength and my Redeemer.

(Psalm 19:14)

"The heart is deceitful above all things,

And desperately wicked;

Who can know it?

I, the Lord, search the heart,

I test the mind,

Even to give every man according to his ways,

According to the fruit of his doings."

(Jeremiah 17:9–10)

Trust in the Lord with all your heart,

And lean not on your own understanding;

In all your ways acknowledge Him,

And He shall direct your paths.

(Proverbs 3:5–6)

Jesus said to him, "'You shall love the Lord your God with all your heart, with all your soul, and with all your mind.'"

(Matthew 22:37)

The wise in heart will receive commands,

But a prating fool will fall.

(Proverbs 10:8)

"You have heard that it was said to those of old, 'You shall not commit adultery.' But I say to you that whoever looks at a woman to lust for her has already committed adultery with her in his heart."

(Matthew 5:27–28)

Your word I have hidden in my heart,

That I might not sin against You.

(Psalm 119:11)

We have all heard it said in today's popular culture that we should just be true to our hearts. This is both poor advice and the opposite of Scripture. The last thing we should ever do is be true to our hearts. Our hearts are deceptive and weak and easily swayed. Rather than being true to our hearts, we should be true to the infallible Word of God. In fact, when we submit ourselves in obedience to the Word of God, our souls fall in line.

Commit your works to the Lord,

And your thoughts [mind, emotion, heart, soul] will be established.

(Proverbs 16:3)

Rather than waiting for the right feeling to do what God says, we should move in swift obedience and watch as our souls (our thoughts and emotions) fall into line. This Scripture teaches us that obedience to God is the pathway to mental and emotional stability.

We understand that our lives are not our own, and we reciprocate His intentions towards us by presenting ourselves fully and daily to Him. This is the first step

OBEDIENCE TO GOD IS THE PATHWAY TO MENTAL AND EMOTIONAL STABILITY.

towards resisting the conforming pressures of both our flesh and the culture we live in. Let's now look at what it means to live in a way that does not conform to the world but lives in alignment with the standards of Heaven.

CHAPTER 16:

DO NOT BE CONFORMED

MARK RAMSEY

Our motivations are, in essence, what informs our allegiances, our loyalties and our influences. We are not to be conformed to the world, meaning that we are not to be motivated or enticed by its trappings or influenced by its value systems. We are to assess our motives and renew our minds so they align with the plans and purposes of Heaven.

We established earlier that a foundational concept of self-leadership in the Kingdom is our identity as sons and daughters of God. We recognise that we are planned and purposed by our Heavenly Father; we are

THERE MUST BE SOMETHING DIFFERENT ABOUT US; WE CANNOT CONFORM TO THIS WORLD. WE MUST REPRESENT ANOTHER WORLD—HEAVEN.

ambassadors of Heaven on earth and commissioned to extend the heart of God into our generation.[1] There must be something different about us; we cannot conform to this world. We must represent another world—Heaven.

OWN A SENSE OF CALLING AND DESTINY

Destiny is not just an idea. Calling is not a vacant or impotent concept. Destiny and calling come from a sense deep down that motivates and drives every high-functioning and high-performing person in the Kingdom of Heaven. They utterly believe in the cause. In the Kingdom, this kind of person is resolutely convinced that God intends to and will use them.

Many Christians ask the wrong questions about becoming involved with Kingdom purposes. They ask things like, "What is in it for me?" and "What do I get out of it?" These are the wrong questions. The answers to these questions are like sugar for the soul—they give you a quick high and fill you for a while but very soon result in a low and leave you hungry again, spiritually malnourished and worse off than before.

The right questions are more like, "Who will I become?" and "What difference will I make?" "What contribution will I make?" "Will my life count in eternity?" "How can I deploy the talents deposited into my life by God?"

These are the Kingdom-minded and others-oriented questions, much like a spiritual protein that sustains our efforts. What is more, when you are the type of person who can ask those questions, then you are more likely to safeguard yourself from becoming a lonely prima donna who no one wants to follow.

Miraculously, when we are more concerned with the significance of our impact for the purposes of Heaven than our own fame and prominence, then the "What will I get?" falls into place as well. The Lord is just that good!

The Bible tells us that if we seek God's ways first, before our own preferences and desires, then the rest will be added or attracted to us as well.

> "But seek first the kingdom of God and His righteousness, and all these things shall be added to you."
>
> (Matthew 6:33)

If we are living wholeheartedly every day for Kingdom purposes and not for our own agendas, then our needs will be met as well; you will never have to worry about what is in it for you when your heart is correctly positioned in submission to God. He is a good Father who cares and provides for His children.

> Also I heard the voice of the Lord, saying:
>
> "Whom shall I send,
>
> And who will go for Us?"
>
> Then I said, "Here am I! Send me."
>
> (Isaiah 6:8)

Isaiah's response to God's call was, "Here I am, send me." His response was not, "Does that include a mobile phone and fuel allowance?" People who own a sense of calling and destiny ask the right questions and exhibit the correct default responses.

Kingdom-minded leaders are not in it for something; they are in it for who they become. They don't conform to the patterns of this world; they want to become who God intended them to become. They believe the cause. They own a sense of calling towards that cause. Their posture says, "God has called me, assigned me and will use me; what an honour!"

A sense of calling and destiny is always stronger than the pain or discouragement you will face along the way. If you do not have that sense of destiny and you inevitably hit the

A SENSE OF CALLING AND DESTINY IS ALWAYS STRONGER THAN THE PAIN OR DISCOURAGEMENT YOU WILL FACE ALONG THE WAY.

barriers of discouragement, hardship, heartbreak and challenge, you simply will not have the wherewithal to push through. You will suddenly and crudely learn that you have been feeding on sugary substitutes instead of your true calling.

However, if you own the call, it will always be stronger than the pain you go through:

You will not be conformed by the challenges you face.
You will be immune to offence.
You will see obstacles as opportunities.
You will possess the clout to push through.
You will cultivate the spiritual fruit of perseverance.
You will become unstoppable.

THE WHY BEHIND THE WHAT

KAROLINA GUNSSER

The first part of being conformed to the will of God is learning, accepting and stewarding a sense of destiny; it is knowing that you are here on purpose for a purpose. The immediate flow-on from that revelation is reconciling the purpose itself. It is one thing to know that you are called; it is another thing to know why.

IT IS ONE THING TO KNOW THAT YOU ARE CALLED; IT IS ANOTHER THING TO KNOW WHY.

We must be able to answer the questions, "Why do I do what I do? Why do I turn up at my workplace, to my career, family, Church and connect group? Why do I lead?"

What is the "why" behind your "what"?[2]

The answer to this question is often convoluted and over-complicated. From the high-school student to the CEO, we have all heard people agonise over calling and purpose, seeking to validate their efforts. It is not as difficult as we have made it out to be. In the Kingdom of Heaven, it is about people.

People.
That is it.
People.

**IN THE KINGDOM,
THE BOTTOM LINE
IS AN ETERNAL
HUMAN VALUE.**

In the corporate world, we are led to believe that the bottom line is a monetary value. In the Kingdom, the bottom line is an eternal human value. God's economy is relationship. Our Saviour, Jesus, summarised all 1,189 chapters of the Bible into two simple statements:

Love God.
Love others.[3]

Now imagine God in Heaven, creating each son and daughter with this specific purpose in mind. He assigns gift sets, personalities and abilities. He chooses the time and season. He delivers that child to its generation as an answer, crafted strategically into a time and community, then steps back. All of Heaven waits with bated breath as they watch this son or this daughter navigate their unique purpose in their design.[4]

Some of us have mistaken the "why" for things other than the love of God and the love of people. We have celebrated the gift set and talents themselves or have lived lives deploying those talents for selfish gain. Some of us have forfeited, resigned and conceded defeat, living each day with very little purpose at all.

Let us remind you today that you are potent with potential. You are powerful. You are dynamic. You are a force to be reckoned with. You are here on purpose for a purpose. Whichever sphere of influence God has you in right now, that purpose is quite simply, people.

In Church life, our "why" is seeing individuals come in off the street, bend under the revelation of the Holy Spirit and walk through an amazing transformation in their lives. That is the "why" of the Great Commission and the "why" of every Jesus follower.[5] Even if it were for just one such story each year, it would be worth it. Watching the boundless love of God bring such an all-consuming transformation to a person is to witness the greatest miracle of all. To watch someone who was so unaware of God or in rebellion to Him, now completely immersed in His love and power in their life, is like nothing else in this world. It is a compelling and relentless "why" that we pursue year after year.

What is your motivation? What is your "why"? What is your purpose? If you have a dream, then you are at least responsible to take a hold of that dream and bring it to pass. When you understand that you have been endowed with spiritual gifts for the purpose of bringing Heaven to earth, your "why" becomes clear. You will not worship the gift or the channel for that gift, whether that is a career or a function; you will see clearly that all things lead to one ultimate end—Heaven on earth—and you will understand the contribution your ordained and appointed presence makes to that end.

> "And you shall remember the Lord your God, *for it is He who gives you power* to get wealth, *that He may establish His covenant* which He swore to your fathers, as it is this day."
>
> (Deuteronomy 8:18, emphasis added)

After you discover that your "why" is a unique application of loving God and loving people, you will naturally move beyond that to ask, "How am I helping others step into their 'why'?"

THAT IS LEADERSHIP: MAKING ANOTHER PERSON'S DREAMS COME TRUE.

The true measure of a leader is actually how they help others fulfil their dreams. That is leadership: making another person's dreams come true. That is when you have made it as a leader.

This was the purpose of Abraham's existence—to be a father, a leader and to make a way for God's people on the earth.

This was Moses' mandate—to lead God's people out of a nightmare and in the direction of promise.

This was the measurement of Joshua's success. He was commissioned by Heaven to lead a nation into its future.

This was the mantle on David—to lay up an inheritance for the next generation, to build a habitation for the presence of God.

This was the purpose of Paul's conversion—to train up and mobilise a movement of people who would bring Heaven's power to the earth.

Are you doing that? Are you establishing God's Kingdom on the earth? Are you helping others step into their "why"? How are you doing that?

One of the greatest instigators for motivating and mobilising others into their calling is passion. People respond to passion and conviction. Passion is a great persuader. Passion is contagious. People love to be around it; it is attractive.

PASSION IS A GREAT PERSUADER.

As leaders, we should never make apologies for being passionate or compelled by the dream inside us. We do not have to dull it down. We do not serve ourselves or anyone else by turning down the temperature on our passion when our passion is for the betterment of others. We should live loud and big and on cause. Passion is captivating, and passion changes the world.

I love being around passionate people. I recently signed up at a new gym with a friend, and when we were signing up, the salesperson got talking about nutrition. I quickly got the impression that he could have spoken to us about diet and nutrition for hours. I was so impacted by his conviction that I thought I really should just go home, clean out my fridge and pantry, and make some major life adjustments. His passion was contagious and compelling.

Occasionally when I go out for a run early in the morning, I see all the early risers going for their run. I'm always surprised just how many fit people there are in the world at that time of day—not the ones who fall out of bed just in time to crawl into their car half-dressed and eat breakfast on the way. No, these are the ones who are rising with the sun. That passion is so inspiring.

One of our executive pastors recently went to a darts championship with his son just for a bit of fun. When he told us about the night, we were all surprised to learn that our city's convention centre is filled annually by darts champions.

It always impresses me the various things that people can be passionate about. But the truth is, passion, cause and conviction are things that move other people and inevitably the world.

The most effective leaders in history were the ones who lived and breathed for a cause.

Mother Teresa always comes to mind with the great work among the poor of Calcutta. Martin Luther King stands out for his religious reformation. Bill Gates and Steve Jobs were both compelled to change the world through technological advances.

Winston Churchill, although by no means advocating the life of Hitler, made a comment once that Adolf Hitler was one of the most effective leaders in history, taking Germany from being economically backward to becoming a global economic powerhouse.

Martin Luther King said, "A person not willing to die for a cause is not fit to live." When you walk, talk, eat, sleep and breathe for a cause, it will get you out of bed in the morning, and people will be attracted to it no matter what it is. Figuratively speaking, you will not need an alarm clock because a passion for the cause will call your name each day, and it will stir the hearts of those around you.

YOUR PURPOSE COMPELS OTHERS TO HAVE THEIR OWN PURPOSE.

Your purpose compels others to have their own purpose. Passion is vital to self-leadership.

The question then begs to be asked, "How do I stir passion, and how do I keep it hot?"

The answer is exposure.

THE NEED FOR EXPOSURE

KAROLINA GUNSSER

A sure way to provoke passion is through exposure. There are some things we cannot un-see or un-feel. Exposure can take on many forms.

In the corporate setting, we may identify a common or recurring need within the market that is not being satisfied by any other organisation. For the entrepreneur, this will stir the creative energy required to create a niche product or service.

Countless great humanitarian works and ministries were birthed out of exposure to the need present in the world. Our very own *She Rescue Home* in Cambodia and *IT'S NOT OKAY Projects* began from this exact thing. Our Senior Pastor, Leigh Ramsey, and her sister-in-law, Hilary, were approached by a young child in a cafe in Cambodia who was desperate for help to find her friend who had just been sold by her parents to a man.

This devastating and divine encounter opened our world up to the horrors of present-day human trafficking, and the *She Rescue Home* was born. In 2019, we welcomed our one-hundredth girl into the home; we have seen several babies born in our care to teenage mothers and have re-integrated dozens of girls safely back into their communities after providing health care, education, legal support and micro-enterprise opportunities to their extended families.

That fateful afternoon in the Cambodian coffee shop was the catalyst for passion and change. The weight of responsibility for that one young girl weighed so heavily on Pastor Leigh's heart that she adopted a mantra by Sharon Cohn Wu to keep her focus sharp.

"To succumb to the enormity of the problem is to fail the one" (Sharon Cohn Wu, International Justice Mission).

"TO SUCCUMB TO THE ENORMITY OF THE PROBLEM IS TO FAIL THE ONE."

Exposing ourselves to hurting and broken people will motivate us to act.

When we expose ourselves to need and allow ourselves to truly see, feel and hear the realities of that need, we can be moved towards a cause. There is great need in all sectors of society and all spheres of culture.

It must also be said that we cannot dismiss the need of both the affluent and the marginalised. We are all in need of Christ-centred solutions to problems and challenges. A person living in an affluent society needs Jesus as much as an orphan in the third world. The heart of God extends to them both as His beloved children. The needs are certainly different, but the heart of God towards them both is the same. He will send an answer in the form of you or me. The response and the required passion to bring the answer are always the same—we live to bring more of Heaven to earth so that more of earth can go to Heaven.

WE LIVE TO BRING MORE OF HEAVEN TO EARTH SO THAT MORE OF EARTH CAN GO TO HEAVEN.

We need to allow ourselves to feel the brokenness around us so that we can be moved with passion. Let us be like the Good Samaritan, who not only saw the need when exposed to it but also filled that need.[6] For you, it may literally be walking across the street to a neighbour to fulfil a need; to another, it may be a journey across the globe.

Let us consider two valuable impetuses for ongoing passion.

i) SCRIPTURE

Studying Scripture is a sure key to unlocking passion. Scripture is alive and active. Exposure to it has the power to move us. We need to learn and meditate on the promises of God so that we can come to understand our individual place within the greatest cause of all time. You have a place in God's grand story, and you will find clarity for it in the Scriptures.

In the Kingdom, we cannot stir up authentic passion or manufacture it on our own; it has to be a Spirit-breathed conception. Kingdom passion is inextricably connected to individual calling, and so it must be the result of genuine revelation coming from the very breath of God. One of the clearest ways God speaks to us is through His Word; it shapes us, moulds us and aligns our priorities.

Learning the Scriptures teaches us two things about the cause of Heaven:

1. God's heart for humanity—all Scripture is a love story about God reaching out to humankind with a heart of love and salvation.

2. God loves to partner with all kinds of people in His mission—many in Scripture started out as dysfunctional, inadequate, untrained and hesitant. Despite these qualities, God performed great and miraculous exploits in partnership with them according to their obedience and trust.

These two foundations evidenced in Scripture equip us and embolden us. They train us in how the culture of the Kingdom works. They assure us that God is able to move in impossible situations. They teach us "excellence" in both deed and character. They teach us compassion. They teach us faith. They teach us many things relative to the unique calling God has placed inside us.

Consistent exposure to and deep affinity with the Scriptures builds us in the Kingdom and gives us the wherewithal to resist the conforming pressures of the world around us.

ii) OTHERS

As already stated, passion is highly contagious. When discovering your "why" and when desiring to stay focused and effective in it, it is important to surround yourself with other passionate people.

IT IS IMPORTANT TO SURROUND YOURSELF WITH OTHER PASSIONATE PEOPLE. At times, you may need to peel away from the negative and complacent influences in your life and get around some hot-blooded passionate people. Invest in yourself by attending conferences and seminars where you can catch more fire towards the cause you are devoted to. Hear from the voices of those who have gone before you or who can challenge you to go further. Reach out to people who can stir you and enlarge your thinking because of their passion.

Expose yourself to people living whole-heartedly for a great cause—positive people, excited people, people who see opportunity in every problem and people who are living for others.

We will explore the concept of exposure a little further in a later section on coaching. For now, let us commit to exposing ourselves to the potent effects of present needs, Scripture and other passionate people as a means to rising above the standards of the world in which we live. Let us now venture into the exciting prospect of transformation.

CHAPTER 17:

BE TRANSFORMED

KAROLINA GUNSSER

Self-leadership does not happen by accident. People who want to grow in the right direction have to do so on purpose.

Successful people crave understanding, progress and personal development. They are curious, thirsty and hungry to move forward. They are humble, and they are inquisitive. They do not assume that what they don't know isn't worth knowing. They live by the suspicion that there is always more to learn. There is always another question to be asked and another revelation to be had.

LIVE BY THE SUSPICION THAT THERE IS ALWAYS MORE TO LEARN.

Paul revealed this side of himself in his letter to the Church in Corinth when he wrote, "When I was a child, I spoke as a child, I understood as a child, I thought as a child; but when I became a man, I put away childish things" (1 Corinthians 13:11).

He hoped to pass this appetite for growth on to his young apprentice Timothy when writing to him:

> Do not neglect the gift that is in you, which was given to you by prophecy with the laying on of the hands of the eldership. Meditate on these things; give yourself entirely to them, that your progress may be evident to all. Take heed to yourself and to the doctrine. Continue in them, for in doing this you will save both yourself and those who hear you.
>
> (1 Timothy 4:14–16)

In order to grow into maturity, we must be committed to it. It takes effort, focus, grit and perseverance, and there are many tools we can employ towards that plight, things such as training, education and reading literature. We will explore these and other growth pathways in the following sections. As we venture through these concepts, let us keep in mind the reality that the world around us is always moving forward. Therefore, there is no such thing as "staying the same." We are either declining or improving as God and His plans continue to move forward. There is no neutral ground.

PERSONAL GROWTH

Just as building the walls of a city require deliberate action and strategy, so too does the fortification of the soul. We can call this intentionality self-discipline—a term we do not easily embrace. In fact, the employment of self-discipline is required in all three dimensions of leading ourselves—the body, the soul and the spirit. Here in the aspect of the soul, we must learn to develop self-discipline primarily in our thoughts because they affect the outcome of our entire lives.

A) BE DISCIPLINED IN THOUGHT AND ATTITUDE

The Battlefield of the Mind, a well-known book by Joyce Meyer, is a phenomenal and comprehensive overview of how to master the processes and habits of the mind to align with God's design and intent. Joyce challenges us to "think about what we're thinking about."[1] She assures us that we don't have to "own" every thought that drops into our minds but that we can deliberately build healthy thought patterns that will cause our lives to flourish the way God intended them to. This is self-leadership in the secret place of the mind.

The Bible tells us that God has not given us a spirit of fear but of power, love and a sound mind.[2] Some translations say, a "spirit of power, love and self-discipline." Which means a sound mind is consistent with self-discipline. We need to intentionally and resolutely decide or choose what we will and will not allow our minds to dwell on.

A SOUND MIND IS CONSISTENT WITH SELF-DISCIPLINE.

Our minds tell us all sorts of things. Scripture reminds us that our minds can deceive us. We need to diagnose our thoughts correctly because often, our perspectives are not correct. As self-leaders, we need to be able to come into a place where our minds do not dictate to us but where the Word of God dictates the content of our minds.

> For the weapons of our warfare are not carnal but mighty in God for pulling down strongholds, casting down arguments and every high thing that exalts itself against the knowledge of God, bringing every thought into captivity to the obedience of Christ.
>
> (2 Corinthians 10:4–5)

The Apostle Paul is telling us we need to recognise that not every thought that comes into our mind is correct. He instructs us to take every thought captive to the knowledge and truth and reality of Jesus Christ. A self-leader will assess each thought against the Word of God and His promises.

DO NOT OWN A THOUGHT THAT CONTRADICTS GOD, HIS WAYS, HIS WORD OR HIS INTENTIONS!

Several times an hour, we must ask ourselves, "Does this thought line up with what the Lord says about my circumstance, about me, about my future, about the people around me, about His kingdom and about His plans?" If it does not agree with the Word of God, then we must reject it and expel it immediately and ruthlessly from our minds. Do not own a thought that contradicts God, His ways, His Word or His intentions!

Scripture tells us in the first letter to the Church at Corinth that we have the mind of Christ.[3] That is a sobering truth on which to meditate. At the end of every day, we can reflect and consider, "Did I think like Christ today?" With the Spirit alive within us, we are carriers of the presence of God; we have the mind of Christ.

It may require a conscious decision to change from the mind of the flesh to the mind of the Spirit, but that decision is entirely ours to make as we choose whether to lead ourselves or not.

We have to take every thought captive because offence will come, disappointment will come, heartache will come, inadequacy will come, all sorts of thoughts will come against us as we step up to our potential. We need to be able to discipline our thinking in order to live in the way the Scriptures show us we can.

SELF-LEADERSHIP STARTS IN THE MIND.

Self-leadership starts in the mind. Our thoughts lead to attitudes, and our attitudes are pivotal in determining our experiences. A bad attitude can sabotage our destiny. We are responsible for our thoughts and attitudes, and ultimately the fullness of the calling that we walk in.

As in water face reflects face,

So a man's heart reveals the man.

(Proverbs 27:19)

Life throws all sorts of curveballs at us to catch us off guard and get our noses out of joint. We have to guard against those challenges taking root in our hearts and minds so we can avoid fear, bitterness, offence, self-pity and disillusionment. As leaders, we intentionally cultivate discipline around our thoughts and attitudes.

B) BE DISCIPLINED IN WORD

The next area in self-leadership is around our words—what we say. As a leader, you do not have the luxury of being unreliable. Your word is your bond; it is your reputation. When we put our hand up to accept the call to be a leader, we are saying in effect, "I'm going to turn up, and I'm going to do what I say I'm going to do."

Jesus said in Matthew 5 that our "yes" should be "yes" and our "no" be "no" because anything else is from the evil one (see Matthew 5:37). That is reasonably clear and compelling—our words should mean what they say.

Language is critically important to leadership. Consider that the primary function of language was not communication but creation. Just think about the first words ever spoken by God.[4] He used language not to communicate but to create everything that has ever existed.

The primary function of language is creation. What are your words creating? Your words create worlds for you and the people around you. Proverbs tells us that life and death are in the power of the tongue.[5]

THE PRIMARY FUNCTION OF LANGUAGE IS CREATION.

New Testament writer James, addressing the impact of our speech, reminded us that a large ship is steered by a proportionately small rudder, and a tiny steel bit in the mouth of a strong horse controls its movements and behaviours.[6] How we speak over others and ourselves is very powerful.

Let us examine a list of just a few things that Proverbs describes about the power of words and what our words should be.

Our words should be a well of life.[7]
Our words should feed many people.[8]
Our words should build trust with people.[9]
Our words should preserve life.[10]
Our words should turn away anger and wrath and strife.[11]
Our words should be sweet like honeycomb.[12]
Our words should be a tree of life.[13]
Our words should put a stop to gossip.[14]

As leaders, we should always be creating worlds like this for ourselves and the people around us. A self-leader has discipline around their words.

C) BE DISCIPLINED IN DEED

The third area of self-discipline is in our actions. In a culture that can be quite mindless at times, it is significantly important to take *responsibility for* self. We live in a culture that suggests we should just go with the flow—wake up at the crack of noon and make decisions based on the feelings and emotions of the day. Our flesh is happy to entertain this notion. Popular culture can be noticeably indifferent, nonchalant and happenstance. It appears quite often that it is "cool not to care" and that "chill" is in vogue. The dispassionate are often epitomised and influential. But that is not the type of leadership culture or Kingdom culture that is required. Laziness is the way of the flesh; intentionality is the way of the Spirit.

Impartiality and indifference can be the enemy of leadership. It is important that we stand for something, not swayed and tossed by popular culture and ideologies but grounded in truth and conviction.

We should live by the following:

- » Conviction over convenience
- » Purpose over preference
- » Honour over option
- » Passion over popularity

Everybody remembers the man who said, "I have a dream…" (Martin Luther King). No one remembers the person who said, "I've got a bit of a complaint"—and there have been many of them. A dream, or conviction, has action to it; it is moving, advancing and giving others something to join arms with. It may be looking at the same challenge as everyone else, but a dream sees the way through, and action brings it to pass. When we are disciplined in our actions, we know what we believe in and why we believe it, and then we move into action.

Passion is important because it compels us to action. As leaders, we live on purpose for a purpose. We are zealous and calculated in response to that passion. The Prophet Isaiah revealed to us that a generous man devises generous things, and by his generosity, he shall stand.[15] Be encouraged! You have permission to be calculated, to make schemes and devise strategies to bring the plans of God into your generation.

Live by your Kingdom convictions and make schemes to bring them to pass. Be the sort of person who has a vision for what they want to see in the earth and then make plans to bring it to pass. Be a person who acts, and may your actions not be mere reactions.

LIVE BY YOUR KINGDOM CONVICTIONS AND MAKE SCHEMES TO BRING THEM TO PASS.

What we do, we do on purpose. We are intentional. Being *responsible for* self demands we live by conviction, not popular opinion or convenience. When actions are driven by passion, vision and purpose, everything changes in the internal and external world of that person.

We present our whole selves (body, soul and spirit) in our most secret and honest selves, to a place of submission and discipline before God. Self-leadership in the Kingdom recognises that we are *responsible for* ourselves as stewards of all that has been entrusted to us in this life. This approach to self-leadership admits the authority of God and the wisdom and guidance of the Holy Spirit.

D) BE DISCIPLINED IN SPIRIT

We live life from the inside out. The strength of our inner world will determine the longevity and effectiveness of our external efforts. As Christ-followers, the most resolute efforts are to be made first in the realm of the Spirit. We are made in the very image of God; we are Spirit beings, called to lives of power and victory. Yet, many Christians neglect their spiritual lives and their spiritual growth to the detriment of their divine potential and the corresponding impact they are called to have in their generation.

As we lean into the Spirit, we can cultivate His strength in our lives through spiritual disciplines. We will never know God better than we know His Word, and we will never know His Word without the guidance of the Holy Spirit. Discipline in the Word is foundational to our personal growth as followers of Christ. However, there are more avenues of spiritual growth, additional to the study of Scripture.

We may have become familiar with a few of the spiritual disciplines, such as worship, fasting, prayer and studying the Word of God. Other disciplines are less familiar but equally as powerful in our spiritual growth. We may initially be surprised to learn that there are many different spiritual disciplines cited throughout Scripture for us to be aware of and apply to our lives. Additional to the commonly held list, some of the other spiritual disciplines include the following:

1. Celebration
2. Corporate Fellowship
3. Solitude
4. Meditation
5. Service
6. Confession
7. Giving
8. Rest
9. Simplicity[16]

Be encouraged to study these disciplines and strategise how to employ them in your everyday life—this will bring about significant personal growth in your life.

COACHING

As well as being disciplined, we benefit greatly from possessing a teachable posture and accountability. He who grows alone grows weird. One of the best ways to grow healthily is by exposure to big-thinkers and leaders in the fields we seek to grow in. In the Kingdom, we call this discipleship.

Coaching (or discipleship) involves a relationship between two people where one speaks into the life of the other to help strengthen abilities, identify and combat weaknesses, and draw out that person's God-potential.

We see in Scripture that Elisha had Elijah, Timothy had Paul, the disciples had Jesus, Saul had Samuel, Samuel had Eli, and Ruth had Naomi. This is a biblical pattern that involves a mutual investment from both parties. It requires accountability, teachability and long-term commitment.

COACHING (OR DISCIPLESHIP) INVOLVES A RELATIONSHIP BETWEEN TWO PEOPLE WHERE ONE SPEAKS INTO THE LIFE OF THE OTHER TO HELP STRENGTHEN ABILITIES, IDENTIFY AND COMBAT WEAKNESSES, AND DRAW OUT THAT PERSON'S GOD-POTENTIAL.

Put yourself with someone who has runs on the board, with a proven character that you trust. Invite their input, correction and advice. Then apply it.

STRATEGY

Personal growth requires a plan. John Maxwell, in a conference a number of years ago, said, "Growth is not an automatic process; if you're going to grow, you will have to do so intentionally."

Be diligent to improve your strengths and identify and work on your weaknesses. This will probably require a plan because just beating yourself up about weaknesses will not help you grow. A sober-minded action plan makes all the difference towards moving in the right direction.

Perhaps you can focus on one area every thirty days and measure your growth at the end of twelve months. John Maxwell calls this a "Personal Growth Plan." There may be some areas that make it onto your list every year, and that is okay. When we work in step with the Holy Spirit, He takes us from glory to glory, as the Word says in 2 Corinthians 3:18. The path of the righteous grows ever brighter,[17] so let's head in that direction intentionally.

THE HOLY SPIRIT NEVER CONDEMNS, BUT HE DOES CONVICT, AND HIS CONVICTION IS EMPOWERING AS HE REACHES OUT AND PULLS US TOWARDS THE GREATNESS GOD INTENDED FOR US.

The great Apostle Paul urged his young disciple, Timothy, to let his growth be evident to all. Our growth should come from a sense of empowerment with the Holy Spirit. The Holy Spirit never condemns, but He does convict, and His conviction is empowering as He reaches out and pulls us towards the greatness God intended for us.

SETTLE YOUR ACCOUNTS

The ultimate form of self-leadership of the soul is making peace with your Creator, yourself and your place in the world. Many people are chasing possessions and validation from sources that will never satisfy. If we do not anchor our soul correctly, it will lead us to all kinds of wilderness places.

Perhaps one of the greatest lessons we must learn is that our accounts are not with man but with God. Abraham taught us a great deal about this principle. See if you can relate in any way to his story.

» He was a man plucked out of obscurity and favoured by God. Check.
» Blessed by no merit of his own, but only by the supreme goodness of God. Check.
» Called to influence beyond his pedigree. Check.

Are you connecting with the story?

Abraham lived his entire life in pursuit of the Lord. He made a mess of things from time to time, but his heart's desire remained on God's words and closeness with Him.

There were several times where it seemed as though he simply would not ever see the fulfilment of the call on his life. One such instance occurred early on and involved someone dear and close to Abraham—his nephew, Lot. We find the account in Genesis 13.

Called Abram at the time, Abraham had just heard the promise of God for the first time—to leave his homeland and follow the vague but strong direction of the Lord to a new land. Abram packed up his family and possessions and set off. But not before taking his nephew with him.

We do not know why Abram included Lot in the tour. Perhaps it was his yearning father's heart; we cannot be sure, but we do know that Abram provided for the young man and treated him as his own son. He gave him a head-start in life and watched him flourish under his care and generosity.

Over the course of time, when both men continued to prosper, Lot's herdsmen began to quarrel with Abram's herdsmen over pasturelands for their growing flocks. Abram, the ultimate peacemaker, called Lot in for a conversation to settle the disputes between their companies. Taking Lot to a lofty place overlooking the terrain, Abram offered the young man first pick of lands so they could split the assets and finally go separate ways. Lot surveyed the land and chose the best land for himself. This was one of the earliest displays of self-interest found in the Scriptures.

Abram's response was to freely give it away and let him go. He did not allow the self-serving behaviours of another person to skew his posture of generosity. He did not allow the experience of receiving less at the hand of a loved one to shrink his own heart.

Only a short time later, we find Lot in trouble, requiring the assistance of his uncle for rescue. Abram always sought peace. Even after Lot went his own way, Abram continued to cover and protect his nephew, never speaking badly about or exposing the young man.

Here is the clincher of self-leadership: we must understand that people can be opportunistic and will often act out of self-interest, not because they are evil, but because they are human. That can be extremely painful and can affect the health of our hearts.

Like Abram's nephew, Lot, when someone we love walks out on us and takes the best of us with them without even turning around to say "thank you," it can be extremely painful. The problem is that we can then allow ourselves to dwell on the injustice of the situation. We can fall into a cycle of rehearsing the unhealthy narrative.

Abram teaches us that we must keep our hearts pure. We must continue to bless. We must continue to love and cover and live freely with what we have, always remembering that what we have has been given to us by God. It was Abram's ability to live freely before God that kept him in the running for the promise.

SELF-LEADERSHIP REQUIRES A RESOLVE: MY ACCOUNTS ARE WITH GOD, NOT MAN.

Self-leadership requires a resolve: my accounts are with God, not man.

> "And the King will answer and say to them, 'Assuredly, I say to you, inasmuch as you did it to one of the least of these My brethren, you did it to Me.'"
>
> (Matthew 25:40)

This is indeed the measuring stick for anyone who is a true follower of Christ: the ability to serve in all things as unto the Lord. What makes it more pointed is the admission that we simply cannot out-give God. Paul reminded the Church in Rome that there is no person living, or who has ever lived, who has given so much to God that He is indebted to them.[18] He is supremely good and generous at all times and in all seasons. Every experience of trial, challenge, sacrifice and self-denial, when done in worship to the King of Heaven, will be used for the betterment of our destiny.

> And we know that all things work together for good to those who love God, to those who are the called according to His purpose.

(Romans 8:28)

When we remember all these things, we can bring our hearts back into health, sincerity, peace and contentment. Regarding the matters of the heart, we must look to God only and not man; our accounts are held with Him in Heaven, not here on earth. We lead ourselves well when we look to God for validation and reward, not man. Longevity and effective self-leadership require that we settle our accounts well.

Your destiny is in the hands of God, not man. So too is your reward.

Let us now draw together all we have learned and assess where we stand in our expanded leadership journey.

LEADING THE PERSON I AM RESPONSIBLE FOR

PERSONAL REFLECTION:

Secret Sin
Why is it important to be accountable to my leaders?

Vision
What practices can I adopt to ensure
my vision doesn't leak?

Self-Check
How can I make sure I am growing
in self-awareness?

Blind Spots
Why is it important to have my blind spots exposed?

CHAPTER 18:

THE EXPANDED LEADER

MARK RAMSEY AND KAROLINA GUNSSER

When it all comes down to it, we must understand that we are all called to lead at some level. Leadership is not only for the person who carries a formal title or the one who lives at the top of the proverbial ladder. No, every team member carries a valuable leadership function that contributes to the overall. Every person is a leader in some context. When we are committed to leading the people around us in powerful, grace-oriented ways, we will see more of Heaven's power released in the spheres where we have influence.

There truly is no greater privilege than that of influencing another person. It is our call from Heaven—to partner with God in His quest to reach mankind. Whatever vocation we find ourselves in, this mandate remains the same for every Jesus follower.

Our lives make an impact. They are designed to make an impact in Heaven's favour. When we realise that every encounter in our daily experience is designed to be an act of service, our influence as individuals is expanded.

In these pages, we have seen that leadership is multidimensional. We have seen that there is indeed more than one way to lead. When we humbly lead those we are *responsible over*, we model Jesus' servant-hearted approach to people through empowerment. When we lead those we are *responsible with*, we recognise the synergistic effect of peer-leadership and its power to exponentially shift culture and create change. We lead those we are *responsible to* through honour and solution-oriented resolutions. We ultimately underscore our entire leadership expression through a dynamic and honest leadership of self through the empowerment of the Holy Spirit; we lead the only person we will ever be *responsible for*.

The expanded leader is one who leads in every dimension, every sphere, in every setting, with every encounter and with all people. They do it all with a posture of servanthood, as this is the greatest in the Kingdom of Heaven. The expanded leader has recognised the capacity they carry to influence their world for good and for God, no matter where they find themselves or with whom. They are called to bring Heaven's answers into their world.

When recruiting His future leadership team, Jesus said, "Come and follow me, and I will transform you into men who catch people for God" (Matthew 4:19 TPT). As they left their old lives to follow Him, Jesus did indeed do a work of "transforming them" into something new. They became influencers of people across the whole spectrum of society—from civic leaders and authorities, to common everyday people, to social outcasts and the unlovely ones of the day. They were expanded to carry an answer anywhere and everywhere their feet would take them.

There is an "I will transform you" journey for each of us to embark on with Jesus, one that He said He would show us how to navigate by the grace and empowerment only He can offer.[1]

Prayerfully consider and answer the following questions:

Where am I at in my capacity as an expanded leader?

What is the next step of growth for me as I continue to unlock the impact God has ordained for me to make in my spheres of influence?

Which of the four dimensions of leadership covered in this book am I strong in already? Can I strengthen those any further? How will I further expand in those strengths?

In which of the four dimensions of leadership have I identified a shallowness or weakness? What is my plan to expand in those areas?

PERSONAL ASSESSMENT

Following is a Personal Assessment you can complete relating to each of the four dimensions of leadership we have explored in this book. You can score each dimension out of 25 to bring together each of the attributes of *Expanded Leadership* in your life. You can then write the scores in the corresponding boxes on the final diagram.

LEADING THOSE I AM RESPONSIBLE OVER

Scale 1–5
1 = Untrue
5 = Very True

1. I am always willing to serve my team in practical ways.

    _____

2. I am driven more by a person's potential than by my agenda.

    _____

3. I am excited and confident inviting a person to become involved with the mission I lead.

    _____

4. I create space for big thinkers, and I have many of them on my team.

    _____

5. My team has an enthusiastic grasp on how their part impacts the cause because we spend time communicating and celebrating that.

    _____

Score out of 25: _____

LEADING THOSE I AM RESPONSIBLE WITH

Scale 1–5
1 = Untrue
5 = Very True

1. I do not only delegate tasks; I also delegate authority so that team members have a voice in the organisation.

   _____

2. I am always willing to serve in areas that fall outside of my immediate job description or area of responsibility.

   _____

3. I am willing to step out from the crowd to reinforce positive culture.

   _____

4. I am genuinely happy when others are promoted.

   _____

5. I make it a practice to find ways I can contribute to the efforts of others.

   _____

Score out of 25: _____

LEADING THOSE I AM RESPONSIBLE TO

Scale 1–5
1 = Untrue
5 = Very True

1. I never present a problem without already strategising several solutions for it and being willing to take full responsibility for the execution of the action plan.

   _____

2. I am not threatened by challenges; I thrive on being creative and thinking outside the box.

   _____

3. I refuse to be involved in conversations or actions that dishonour my leader or contradict what the Word of God says about authority.

   _____

4. I am aware that the challenges my leaders face are not always known to me, so I do my best to lighten their load.

   _____

5. I am willing to generously offer ideas even if they are not always adopted or I don't receive the credit for them.

   _____

Score out of 25: _____

LEADING THE PERSON I AM RESPONSIBLE FOR

Scale 1–5
1 = Untrue
5 = Very True

1. I admit that I have blind spots, and I have therefore created lines of accountability to help me grow.

_____

2. I intentionally and regularly remind myself that I am serving God and not man, so I don't seek public recognition or human validation.

_____

3. I keep my heart clean as a discipline through a thriving relationship with the Holy Spirit and employing spiritual disciplines.

_____

4. I have a strategic plan for personal growth.

_____

5. I have a strong identity in Christ; I know and live out of what He says about me.

_____

Score out of 25: _____

TOTAL SCORES

These scores are not about passing or failing; they are a tool to help you identify your approach to each of the four dimensions of *Expanded Leadership*. After doing this simple assessment, you might wish to go back over the relevant sections of this book and make a practical growth strategy for the areas you want to address.

May your leadership journey begin today and bear much eternal fruit in the future for the Kingdom of God.

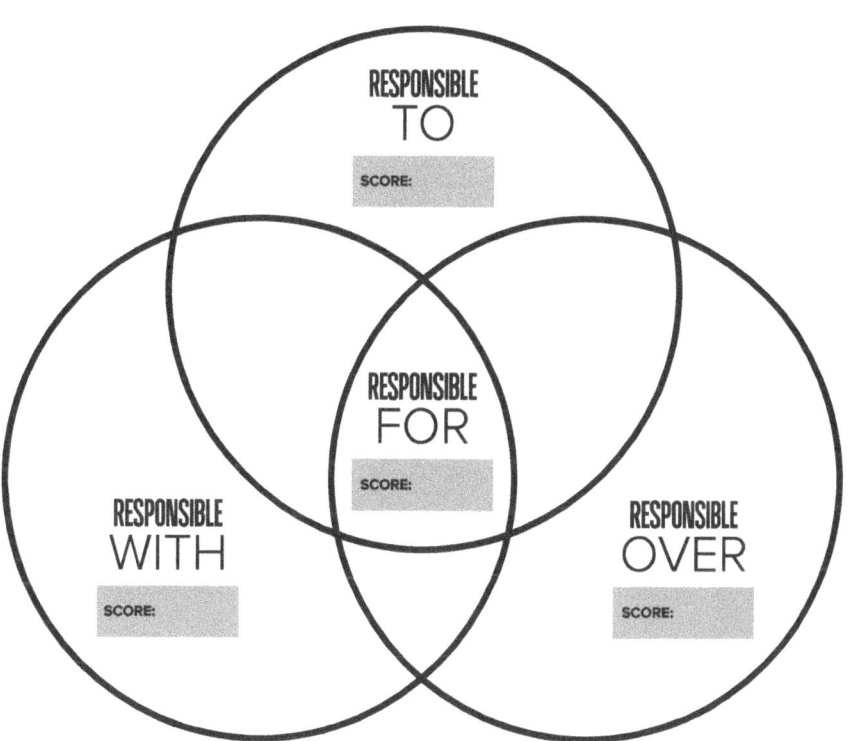

NOTES

PROLOGUE

[1] Trent Shelton, "56 Best Trent Shelton Quotes and Thoughts" *Brilliant Read.* https://www.brilliantread.com/56-best-trent-shelton-quotes-and-thoughts/ (accessed February 18, 2021).

CHAPTER 1: DISPELLING THE MYTH

[1] Matthew 5: 14–16
[2] Maxwell, J C 2005, *The 360 Degree Leader: Developing Your Influence from Anywhere in the Organisation*, Nelson Business, Nashville.

CHAPTER 2: RULES OF ENGAGEMENT

[1] Matthew 7:1–2
[2] Matthew 14: 22–33
[3] James 1:8
[4] Proverbs 3:34, James 4:6, 1 Peter 5:5
[5] Proverbs 18:6–7
[6] Romans 10:9–10
[7] Hebrews 4:1–3

PART ONE: LEADING THOSE I AM RESPONSIBLE OVER
CHAPTER 3: RESPONSIBLE OVER

1. Matthew 25:21–23
2. 1 Peter 5:2–4

CHAPTER 4: EMPOWER PEOPLE

1. Matthew 7:16–20

CHAPTER 5: IRRESISTIBLE ENVIRONMENTS

1. Genesis 22:2; John 3:16
2. John 16:7
3. 2 Chronicles 7:14; James 5:15
4. Malachi 3:10–12
5. Maxwell, JC 2007, *Be a People Person: Effective Leadership Through Effective Relationships*, 2nd edn, David C Cook, Colorado Springs, CO.
   a. In-text citation—page 76
6. Proverbs 18:16
7. 2 Timothy 4:7

PART TWO: LEADING THOSE I AM RESPONSIBLE WITH
CHAPTER 7: ACTIVATING THE SILENT MAJORITY

1. Chand, S 2016, *What's Shaking Your Ladder?: 15 Challenges All Leaders Face*, Whitaker House, New Kensington, PA.
2. Luke 10:1–20
3. John 14:12
4. Matthew 28:16–20
5. Maxwell, J 2019, *Become a Leader Others Want to Follow*, https://www.johnmaxwell.com/blog/become-a-leader-others-want-to-follow/ [Accessed 10/09/2019].
6. Carnegie, D 1981, *How to Win Friends and Influence People*, Simon and Schuster, New York, NY.

CHAPTER 8: CELEBRATE

1. Exodus 20:17
2. Luke 1:28–33 paraphrased
3. Matthew 14:22–33, John 18:10, Matthew 26:35, Matthew 16:23, John 13:23

CHAPTER 9: STEPPING OUT FROM THE CROWD

1   2 Samuel 23:8–39
2   Philippians 3:14, 1 Corinthians 11:1
3   Wilson, L 2019, *Sustaining Workforce Engagement: How to Ensure Your Employees Are Healthy, Happy, and Productive*, Routledge/Productivity Press, New York, NY.
    a. In-text citation – page 422
4   Romans 8:37
5   Deuteronomy 28:13
6   1 Samuel 17:28
7   1 Samuel 18:6–7
8   Genesis 37:18–36, Genesis 39:1–23
9   Romans 5:8, Hebrews 10:12–14
10 Maxwell, JC 2013, *Be a People Person: Effective Leadership Through Effective Relationships*, David C Cook, Colorado Springs, CO.
    b. In-text citation – page 75

PART THREE: LEADING THOSE I AM RESPONSIBLE TO
CHAPTER 11: THE POWER OF SECOND

1   1 Peter 5:12, Acts 15:40–41, Acts 16:19–40
2   Romans 8:14–17
3   Numbers 20:1–13, 1 Samuel 13:7–14
4   1 Samuel 24:1–7
5   Bevere, J 2007, *Honor's Reward: How to Attract God's Favor and Blessing*, 1st edn, FaithWords Hachette Book Group, New York, NY.
6   Genesis 18:1–10, Hebrews 13:2
7   Genesis 13:8–12
8   Genesis 14:18–20
9   Proverbs 11:24–25

CHAPTER 12: BE A PROBLEM SOLVER

1   Proverbs 15:20
2   2 Peter 1:3
3   Kotter, JP 2008, A *Sense of Urgency,* Harvard Business School of Publishing, Boston, MA.
4   Matthew 23:11–12

5 Proverbs 6:4, Proverbs 12:24, Proverbs 10:4, Proverbs 27:23, Proverbs 21:5

CHAPTER 13: GIVE HONOUR

1 Proverbs 18:21
2 John 10:10

PART FOUR: LEADING THE PERSON I AM RESPONSIBLE FOR
CHAPTER 14: THE PERSON IN THE MIRROR

1 Matthew 25:21–23
2 1 Kings 11:4, 1 Kings 15:3, 1 Kings 15:14, 2 Kings 18:6
3 Philippians 2:12
4 2 Corinthians 3:18
5 Ephesians 2:10

CHAPTER 15: PRESENT YOURSELF

1 MacDonald, G 2012, *Ordering Your Private World*, Thomas Nelson Publishing, Nashville, TN.

CHAPTER 16: DO NOT BE CONFORMED

1 2 Corinthians 5:20
2 Sinek, S 2011, *Start with Why: How Great Leaders Inspire Everyone to Take Action*, Penguin Group, New York, NY.
3 Matthew 22:36–40
4 Romans 8:19
5 Matthew 28:16–20
6 Luke 10:25–37

CHAPTER 17: BE TRANSFORMED

1 Meyer, J 2002, *Battlefield of the Mind: Winning the Battle in Your Mind*, Warner Faith, New York, NY.
2 2 Timothy 1:7
3 1 Corinthians 2:16
4 Genesis 1:3
5 Proverbs 18:21
6 James 3:4
7 Proverbs 10:11
8 Proverbs 10:21

9   Proverbs 11:13

10 Proverbs 18:21

11 Proverbs 15:1

12 Proverbs 16:24

13 Proverbs 15:4

14 Proverbs 11:13

15 Isaiah 32:8

16 Joshua 1:8, Hebrews 12:28, 1 Thessalonians 5:17, Joel 2:12, Deuteronomy 16:11–14, Hebrews 10:25, Luke 5:16, Matthew 6:6, Philippians 4:8, 1 Peter 4:10, Proverbs 28:13, James 5:16, 2 Corinthians 8:7, 2 Corinthians 9:11, Exodus 34:21, Matthew 6:33

17 Proverbs 4:18

18 Romans 11:35

CHAPTER 18: THE EXPANDED LEADER

1   Matthew 11:28–30

MARK RAMSEY

Since 2000, Mark has led Citipointe Church as it has flourished from one influential location in Brisbane into a global church spanning four nations and thousands of members. Mark has also authored *Spiritually Transmitted Diseases*, a book aimed to equip people to become carriers of healthy, powerful, life-enhancing truths. Passionate about developing the leadership potential in both people and organisations, he oversees more than 650 paid staff members across the world.

Additionally, Mark is the Executive Chairman of Red Frogs Chaplaincy Network, It's Not Ok Projects combatting human trafficking, and Citipointe Christian College, an academically and spiritually excellent K-12 school. Citipointe Church has also birthed Citipointe Worship, the SheRescue Home in Cambodia and Citipointe Ministry College. However, Mark's greatest pride and achievement is in leading his family first. He and his wife Leigh have four beautiful children from their marriage of almost four decades: Josh (and his wife Amy-Jane), Becky (and her husband Aaron), Joel (and his wife Savannah) and Mitch. Adding to the fun are grandchildren Jahi, Sienna, Bam-Bam, Halo, River-Leigh, Avila and Jack. Whether pioneering at home or across the world, Mark wants to equip you with *Expanded Leadership*.

marklramsey.com

KAROLINA GUNSSER

Karolina Gunsser is an anointed Christian voice coming out of Australia. As an author, preacher, blogger and pastor, her influence and ministry are a blessing to many generations across all sectors of society. Combining a background in media, communications and business, years of lived leadership experience and her prophetic edge, Karolina is a strategic thinker and a spiritual architect. She has a powerful communicative ability, which is undergirded by a deep devotion to biblical truth. Her words, both written and orated, deliver revelation and empowerment to audiences around the world.

Alongside her husband Sam, she has been leading teams in churches for more than two decades. Currently they lead the Redcliffe location of Citipointe Church, with a contagious passion and undeniable skill for developing strong layers of leaders and volunteers. Together they are the proud parents to their four champions: Maja Gabrielle, Layla Justice, Judah Cruz and Jesse Jons.

B.Bus (IntBus) B.A. (Jour)

karolinagunsser.com

CITIPOINTE CHURCH

What began as a group of twenty-five people meeting as a homegroup quickly became one of the fastest-growing churches in Australia—seeing hundreds of people added each year to this new way of doing Church. Citipointe is now global, with numerous locations across Australia, New Zealand, Europe, the USA, and over twelve thousand people now call Citipointe their home. Citipointe Church is now one of Australia's largest and most influential churches with the mission to "unmistakably influence our world for good and for God."

We are a contemporary Church grounded in eternal truths.
We have a modern expression to a timeless faith.
We believe the answer to all of life's questions is simply Jesus.
We exist to see people find Christ as their Saviour and then take Him into their world.
We are about bringing glory to God, greatness to His Church and value to the individual.

citipointechurch.com

IT'S NOT OK PROJECTS / SHE RESCUE HOME

Fighting Injustice. Alleviating Poverty. Restoring Lives.

To be free from exploitation in all its forms is a fundamental human right. It's Not Ok Projects stand up against the injustices of poverty, sexual exploitation and human trafficking by restoring the lives of those affected and by replacing vulnerabilities with opportunities for hope. Our projects exist to restore, educate, equip and provide hope to the oppressed, the vulnerable, the impoverished and the at-risk. It's Not Ok Projects includes the SHE Rescue Home and Sewing Centre in Phnom Penh, Cambodia.

itsnotok.com

RED FROGS

We recognise that the culture of young people is dominated by alcohol and that excessive consumption of alcohol and other substances can lead to dangerous and life-altering behaviours. Therefore, we've made it our mission to provide a positive peer presence in alcohol-fuelled environments where young people gather, educate young people on safe partying behaviours and promote alcohol-free and/or diversionary activities that engage young people in these environments. Our vision: to reduce suffering and safeguard a generation of young people, acting as a positive peer presence to empower them to make positive life choices and become a voice of change within their culture.

redfrogs.com.au

CITIPOINTE WORSHIP

There is a sound that rises from our House that brings glory to our God. Citipointe Worship (formerly known as Citipointe Live) is the prophetic sound and worship expression of Citipointe Church, with a desire to magnify Jesus and lead people into a deeper intimacy with Him. Citipointe Worship has expanded into a global expression of the Citipointe Church heartbeat—to unmistakably influence our world for good and for God and continues to see millions across the globe set free through powerful praise and worship songs that bring Heaven to earth.

citipointeworship.com

NOTES

NOTES

NOTES

NOTES

NOTES